Level 7 Leadership

Level 7 Leadership

The Blueprint for the Human+Machine Era

JACK C. SWIFT

Ⱥ

A AUTHOR.INC

Edited by Catt Editing LLC

Cover design by Pete Garceau

Interior design by Zoe Norvell

Hardcover: 978-1-966372-10-3

Paperback: 978-1-966372-55-4

eBook: 978-1-966372-24-0

Audiobook: 978-1-966372-25-7

Published by Author.Inc

Printed in the United States of America

First Edition: March 2026

For more information, visit: www.jackcswift.com

To Lisa, Aiden, Bella, Atticus, and Zephyr,
my greatest teachers in love, presence,
and what truly matters.

L 7 AGENT - BRINGING THE BOOK TO LIFE

This Agent brings *Level 7 Leadership* to life by turning the ideas in the book into practical support you can use in real moments. It helps founders, executives, and entrepreneurs think through specific situations they're facing—on their own or with their teams—by offering personalized prompts, templates, exercises, and thoughtful perspectives. With each interaction, the partnership deepens: humans bring imagination and context, the machine adds structure and precision, and together they accelerate learning, clarity, and results across the organization.

TABLE OF CONTENTS

The Breath Before the Wave

E very era begins with a breath. Before the storm breaks or the tide shifts, there is a stillness—a pause so subtle that only those paying deep attention can sense it. History always announces itself first as silence. The leaders who notice that silence before the noise shape what comes next.

We are living in such a pause now. Civilization itself is drawing breath. Beneath the hum of algorithms and the pulse of markets, something immense is gathering—a convergence of human and machine intelligence, of biology and code, of consciousness and computation. The question is no longer *if* it will arrive, but *whether* we will meet it with full awareness of the moment.

For much of modern history, leadership was measured by control: forecasting, planning, optimizing. The leader served as the center of certainty in a volatile world. But certainty has become the rarest resource of all. Artificial intelligence (AI) evolves faster than any org chart can adapt. Climate, culture, and capital now shift together in real time. The pace of change has outstripped the pace of comprehension. As Einstein warned, we face problems that can no longer be solved by the same thinking that created them.

This book begins at the moment that realization takes hold: on the threshold between epochs.

The Civilizational Turning Point

Every few centuries, humanity rewires its operating system. The printing press democratized knowledge. The steam engine redefined labor. The microchip compressed time and space. Now, artificial intelligence signals more than a technological leap. It reveals a transformation in human consciousness itself, a mirror held to the collective mind.

AI reflects our deepest impulse: to extend ourselves. Every machine, from clock to computer to neural net, externalizes a layer of human capability. What began as muscle became mechanical. What began as reason becomes digital. The next frontier is not smarter machines but more conscious humans: leaders who can sense, interpret, and co-create with intelligence in all its forms.

We stand at what Thomas Kuhn, author of *The Structure of Scientific Revolutions*, might call a paradigm threshold. The old worldview—linear, hierarchical, control-driven—no longer explains the data of experience. The new one is emergent, networked, relational. It values awareness as much as analysis, rhythm as much as rigor. The Level 7 leader does not command from above but participates from within, cultivating coherence across mind, body, team, and technology.

Why Leadership Must Evolve

If the Industrial Age rewarded efficiency, the Intelligence Age rewards attunement—the process of bringing systems into harmony. Traditional models were built for prediction in stable systems. Today's environment is anything but— fluid, nonlinear, paradoxical. A single decision now ripples globally in seconds.

This new terrain demands a different kind of nervous system: a leadership physiology, not just a philosophy. Stress resilience, emotional regulation, and interoceptive awareness are now strategic assets. Neuroscience confirms what contemplative traditions have long known: A leader's state shapes the state of the system. A calm nervous system transmits coherence. A reactive one multiplies noise.

Level 7 leadership proposes that transformation at scale begins not with structure, but with state. When leaders shift from control to coherence, from ego to ecosystem, organizations begin to breathe differently. Meetings shorten. Innovation accelerates. Trust compounds. The invisible architecture changes. The collective rhythm shifts and somehow feels less effortful.

Definition of Level 7 Leadership

Level 7 leadership is an evolved operating system for the human+machine era, where intelligence is both biological and artificial, where change accelerates exponentially, and where leadership is no longer defined by control but by coherence. It is the next octave of leadership, built upon the foundations of earlier frameworks but designed for a world moving faster than linear thinking can process. **There are no preceding six levels. The name "Level 7" stands alone** and is meant to represent the fully embodied leader, operating at this new level.

In Level 7 leadership, human and machine intelligence form a single integrated team. Humans bring imagination, intuition, creativity, emotional intelligence, meaning-making, and adaptability—the capacities that cannot be automated. Machines bring speed, precision, memory, pattern recognition, and scale—the capabilities humans cannot sustain. Separately, each is powerful. Together, when harmonized by a Level 7 leader, they become the most effective and efficient leadership system ever evolved.

Level 7 leadership recognizes that in environments of compounding complexity, people do not follow titles; they follow presence. The Level 7 leader sets energetic, emotional, and narrative coherence across the system. They sense emerging patterns before they are obvious, combine intuitive knowledge with machine-generated insight, and create the conditions in which both human potential and technological capability can flourish. They understand that machines amplify whatever the leader transmits—vision or fear, coherence or chaos. Therefore, the leader's inner life becomes a strategic asset.

The Level 7 leader is the architect of the human+machine team.

They are human enough to imagine what doesn't yet exist.

Technological enough to wield the intelligence now available.

Conscious enough to remain grounded amid accelerating change.

Precise enough to convert vision into aligned action.

Humble enough to collaborate with machines.

Courageous enough to reinvent themselves continuously.

Level 7 leadership is not about reducing uncertainty, but transforming it into creative possibility. It is not about commanding the system, but tuning it. It is not about outworking complexity, but out-sensing it. It is the shift from control to coherence, from hero-based leadership to system-based intelligence, from human-versus-machine to human+machine as a single evolutionary step.

Level 7 leadership is the blueprint.

The Level 7 leader is the embodiment.

The human+machine team is the path forward.

From Order → Disorder → Reorder

This book follows the rhythm of life itself: order, disorder, reorder.

Part I—Order: The inhale explores the foundations of leadership as we've known it—its assumptions, strengths, and limits. We examine why even noble models, like servant leadership, strain under exponential complexity.

Part II—Disorder: The opening enters the crucible of transformation, where old certainties dissolve and sensing replaces strategy. Here, neuroscience, psychology, and organizational design converge to reveal that chaos is not the enemy. It is the birthplace of innovation.

Part III—Reorder: The return integrates the lessons of both. It reimagines leadership as a living ecosystem: humans and machines in dynamic coherence, guided by rhythm, story, and shared meaning.

This cyclical arc mirrors nature's intelligence: inhale, exhale, pause. Every breakdown is a prelude to breakthrough. Every collapse composts the ground for renewal. At its highest form, leadership echoes this biological truth.

The Core Premise: Coherence as Competence

Across disciplines, from physics to physiology, a single principle recurs: coherence. Systems thrive when their parts resonate in rhythm. They fragment when signals compete. The same holds for teams, organizations, and consciousness itself.

A Level 7 leader cultivates coherence on three levels:

- **Inner coherence:** A nervous system aligned across head, heart, and gut, with decisions made from presence, not panic

- **Relational coherence:** Teams that trust, communicate, and entrain around shared intent, not hierarchy
- **Systemic coherence:** Organizations that learn in real time, blending human intuition with machine precision

This is not soft science. It is a survival strategy. Complexity will only escalate. The only structure that survives is a living one—able to sense, adapt, and regenerate.

From Human vs. Machine → Human+Machine

Too much of today's AI conversation is stuck in the language of competition: human *versus* machine, carbon *versus* silicon. That frame is too small for what's unfolding. The deeper opportunity is symbiosis.

As mentioned in the definition of Level 7 leadership, when machines calculate, humans can contemplate. When algorithms accelerate, humans can attune. Leadership becomes the orchestration of both: data's velocity joined to discernment's depth.

A Book for Those Who Sense the Shift

This book is for leaders who feel the ground shifting. Who know spreadsheets alone can't explain the future. It is for the founders, executives, and change-makers who sense that intuition is data, that culture is code, and that the most vital operating system to upgrade is the human one.

There is no rigid formula here. Only patterns, principles, and embodied practices. This book contains tools: breathing protocols, decision audits, energy check-ins. For coherence is not a theory to accept, but a state to be practiced.

The Invitation

The breath before the wave is sacred. It invites us to feel the widening field between what has been and what could be. Leadership in the age of AI is not about commanding the tide. It is about learning to surf it with awareness.

This book is that practice. It will challenge instincts toward control. It will reward curiosity over certainty. And it will reveal that resilience is rhythm made visible. Here you'll find science and story, data and philosophy, all woven to prove a single truth: Consciousness, not code, is the ultimate lever of transformation.

As you read, pause often. Breathe. Notice what shifts within you. The Level 7 leader is not a title to earn. It is a frequency to embody.

The next renaissance will not be painted on canvas or printed in ink. It will be composed in the medium of awareness itself.

Take one full breath.

The wave is already rising.

Let's begin.

CHAPTER 1

The Civilizational Turning Point

"A new type of thinking is essential if mankind is to survive and move toward higher levels."—*Albert Einstein*

We are at a civilizational inflection point: Beneath apparent stability, foundational shifts are underway. The Fourth Industrial Revolution is not merely technological change; it is a profound civilizational turning point that requires new patterns of perception and leadership. Our ability to decode these patterns and respond effectively will define our collective future.

The outward signs of progress—skyscrapers, markets, and global influence—can mask a subtler transformation. The scaffolding of our civilization is softening, almost imperceptibly. Leadership now demands that we sense this transition and orient toward what is emerging.

Society's tectonic plates are in motion, invisibly reshaping our world. Old systems of leadership, economics, education, and meaning from the Industrial Age are breaking under relentless change. As Klaus Schwab, founder and executive of the World Economic Forum (WEF) said, "The Intelligent Age . . . is a societal revolution, one that has the power to elevate humanity or indeed fracture it."[1] He also termed this period the Fourth Industrial Revolution.

Collapse is half the story. Every breakdown clears the way for emergence. Disorder signals a threshold in the cycle of order, disorder, and reorder. The question is, "Who are the leaders sensing patterns and guiding us into the future?"

It is clearly a time for a new leadership mindset and methodology.

A Renaissance in Disguise

Every leap in history required a reinvention of our collective story. Historian Yuval Noah Harari notes that civilizations are built as much on narrative as on stone. From the Cognitive Revolution to silicon chips, each era arrived with new machines and a new need for meaning-making.

The Renaissance of the fifteenth and sixteenth centuries offers a powerful precedent. Europe had endured centuries of plague, war, and rigid hierarchy. Collapse was the dominant note. Yet from that disorder emerged one of humanity's most fertile eras:

- **Artistic revolution:** Linear perspective transformed how humans saw reality. Michelangelo and Leonardo da Vinci rendered the human form with sacred dignity, blending science and art in ways that remain timeless.
- **Scientific revolution:** Copernicus and Galileo displaced the Earth from the center of the cosmos, shattering certainty and opening vast space for discovery.
- **Philosophical revolution:** Humanism placed value on the dignity and potential of the individual, breaking from dogma.
- **Exploratory revolution:** New continents were mapped, horizons expanded, and imagination leapt with them.
- **Institutional revolution:** Universities, democratic experiments, and modern banking systems were seeded, institutions that still shape our lives centuries later.

The Renaissance was chaotic. Yet from disorder emerged modern science, governance, democracy, and belief in human potential. Collapse birthed creativity.

And who led the way? The creatives: artists, explorers, scientists, and visionaries who could imagine differently. They stood at the edge of collapse and painted, built, discovered, and wrote their way into a new order.

Collapse is not a finish line but an opening. As the old systems recede, a new Renaissance, defined by transformative technology and new mindsets, quietly gathers on the horizon. Those who can sense emerging patterns and co-create with AI are poised to chart the course into this next era. This is the central challenge and promise of our current turning point.

Exponential Disruption: The Compression of Time

Every seismic shift in history shares one hallmark: speed.

From horse to car. In 1900, there were more horses than cars on New York City's streets. By 1913, Ford's assembly line cut the Model T's price in half. By the 1920s, horses had largely disappeared from urban life. A millennia-old mode of transport evaporated in less than two decades.

From landlines to mobile. In 2011, 35% of US adults owned a smartphone; today, about 91% do. In just over a decade, we went from checking email at a desk to carrying the world's knowledge, and a personal AI assistant, in our pockets.

From stigma to standard in dating. In 1995, online dating was a curiosity. Today, more than 40% of heterosexual and 60% of same-sex relationships begin on an app.

The lesson was never about tools, but adaptability. Institutions sure of their permanence shifted in weeks. Established systems proved fragile when time compressed.

According to McKinsey, 78% of organizations now use AI in at least one business function, and the use of generative AI nearly doubled in 2024.[2] Executives report not only cost savings but entirely new revenue streams. The curve is steepening.

For leaders, disruption is certain. In this accelerated era, adaptability and awareness are the new currency of effectiveness.

The River Mindset: Strength in Flow

History is a river. Leadership once followed a slow, predictable stream. Then the river hits a drop or flood. Still waters become rapids.

Water teaches—sometimes gentle, often powerful, always unstoppable. Like a patient artist, it carves canyons, moves stone, and reshapes landscapes not by force, but by persistence and flow.

We live in a flooded river era, where change surges. There's no holding back. We must learn to move with the flow.

Level 7 leaders lead like rivers. They're adaptive and resilient, shaping new channels with speed and grace. Floods unsettle, but they also fertilize. Like the Nile renewed Egypt, today's surges nourish possibility.

The Collapse of the Newtonian Mindset (See Appendix)

For two centuries, leadership was likened to Newtonian physics: predictable, mechanical, hierarchical. Leaders diagnosed, prescribed, and controlled. Organizations became machines made up of people as interchangeable parts.

Modern science shattered that worldview. Quantum mechanics revealed reality as relational, probabilistic, and emergent. Systems theory showed that the whole is more than the sum of its parts. Neuroscientist Dr. Tara Swart demonstrates that the human brain itself behaves this way—plastic, constantly rewiring in response to the environment and attention.

As physicist David Bohm observed, what we experience as reality unfolds from a deeper "implicate order."[3] Life, then, is not machinery to control but a field of possibilities to be navigated and explored with curiosity.

Einstein reminded us, as noted above, that the thinking that created our problems cannot be the thinking that solves them. The old, linear, control-driven mindset is dissolving, clearing space for a new form of leadership—one that is fluid, intuitive, relational, and alive.

As renowned research professor Brené Brown has shown, the trait of vulnerability, the willingness to admit not knowing, or not needing to know better, is not weakness but courage in motion.[4] It is precisely that openness that lets leaders sense what is emerging (new way) rather than defend what was (old way).

Story: Building TIFIN: From Linear to Multi-Vector

When I was the CEO of TIFIN—an AI-driven fintech company focused on financial services with strategic partners like J.P. Morgan, Franklin Templeton, and Morningstar—my initial instinct was linear: one company, reach product-market fit, raise Series B, scale, repeat. Logical. Structured. Newtonian. This is what I had known during my formative professional years at Janus Henderson and later as a co-founder at Pacific Current Group (ASX:PAC).

But the rapid pace of AI made that way of thinking obsolete. By the time a single venture reached Series B, the market would be crowded. My thinking was too slow.

Vinay Nair, TIFIN's chairman at the time, and I had a conversation and asked ourselves, "What if, instead of one company, we built ten in the same time frame?" What if we designed a venture studio as a template for launching fintech companies in parallel rather than in sequence? Vinay had already established momentum with 55ip (later sold to J.P. Morgan).

That is what we did. TIFIN became a venture studio in 2020, simultaneously launching multiple AI-native businesses from 2020 to 2022, a living field of emergence. Our mantra became "Innovation at Speed." This was not a chaotic venture play. We intended for all of our companies to succeed. We had a system, and it worked.

In 2020, the CEO of Rippling, Parker Conrad, coined the term "compound start-up," a single company that is designed from Day 1 to build more than a single product, instead building a portfolio of interconnected products, capabilities, and revenue streams, further reinforcing that multidirectional innovative speed is critical in the AI era.

By 2025, TIFIN had founded more than a dozen companies and divisions, each nested within a living system. TIFIN was not and is not simply building companies; we were reprogramming the operating code of leadership itself.

The Mindset Shift: From Case Studies to Intuition

For much of my career—army officer, Janus Henderson executive, COO, CEO—I was trained to study the past to navigate the future. Business schools, *Harvard Business Review* articles, case studies—all built on extracting principles from yesterday and applying them to tomorrow. Stanford University psychologist Carol Dweck names this the "fixed mindset"—a belief that your human qualities, like intelligence and talent, are static and unchangeable, not open to growth.[5] I realized I had internalized an institutional version, treating the past as the only reliable map. Yet in a world redrawn by AI, the landscape shifts too rapidly for old maps to guide us. We don't need to replicate. We need to forge a new trail.

This echoes the Renaissance of the fifteenth century: Europe, once trapped in scholasticism, was endlessly studying Aristotle. The Renaissance broke the pattern. Creatives experimented, observed, and imagined as they dissected cadavers, drew flying machines, and painted new perspectives.

Leadership today calls for that same spirit of experimentation. It invites us to act before permission, to trust intuition alongside instruction. As futurist Amy Webb observes, the future whispers before it shouts.[6] Level 7 leaders learn to listen at the edges, where data has yet to crystallize into trend lines.

Human+Machine: Toward Co-Creation

The rise of AI does not mark the end of human relevance; it marks the end of human complacency. For generations, we idolized optimization and control—the very traits AI has perfected.

Machines already outperform us at calculation and recall, but, paraphrasing Dr. Fei-Fei Li's perspective on human-centered AI: if we want AI to serve humanity, we must infuse it with humanity—reflecting Li's documented philosophy that AI should embody human values."[7] Empathy, imagination, and moral reasoning remain uniquely human.

The call is not to compete with machines, but to co-create alongside them. We bring intuition, empathy, and vision; machines offer speed, scale, and precision. Together, we form a new kind of creative partnership.

Leadership becomes an act of orchestration, a harmony between intelligences. To do this well requires what neuroscientist and MD Tara Swart calls "neural integration": aligning logic and emotion so the whole self participates in decision-making.[8] The Level 7 leader is both engineer and empath, analyst and artist.

Case Studies: Amazon, Shopify, and OpenAI

By 2025, Amazon had deployed over a million robots in warehouses, creating new models of human+machine collaboration. Robots moved shelves, humans picked items, algorithms optimized routes in real time. Leaders oriented their work to human+machine teams, optimizing the contributions of both humans and machines—not simply individually, but collectively.

Shopify's leadership thrived through its "trust battery" culture, defining how trust is built and depleted in workplace relationships and proving that coherence and empowerment scale faster than control. Trust compounded like interest, producing creative energy that no process manual could enforce.

OpenAI's leaders transitioned the company from a lab to a global platform in under a decade, guided not just by code but also by transparency and curiosity—qualities essential for resilience. Its willingness to learn publicly became its operating advantage.

These examples remind us that technology alone does not reshape the world. It is leadership attuned to sensing, adapting, and co-creating with what is emerging that moves the needle.

Contrast this with legacy retailers like Sears, K-Mart, and Toys "R" Us, which clung to the old maps. They didn't die from technology; they died from leadership inertia.

Reflective Practices for Level 7 Leaders

Development is a practice. Engage in one or more of the practices below to increase your ability to sense, adapt, and co-create with the emergent. Try not to *think* but to *listen*; although they're easily confused, they are very different.

- **Emergence journal:** Each morning, ask yourself, "What wants to happen through me today?" Record without judgment.
- **Edge listening:** Once a week, ask someone outside your circle (a junior teammate, a customer, even an AI assistant), "What are you seeing that I'm not?"
- **Embodied pause:** Before a decision, take three slow breaths. Drop attention from head → heart → gut. Notice what arises. (As Brené

Brown teaches, this pause is the birthplace of courage.)

- **Nature calibration:** Once a month, walk in nature with no agenda. Let its rhythm reset your nervous system.
- **Energy audit:** At week's end, note where your leadership left you energized and where it drained. Patterns appear quickly. Ask yourself, "What was I doing? With whom?"
- **Sketch the future:** Channel your inner Leonardo da Vinci and capture one vision of what could be through drawing or writing. These are not optional skills; they are survival skills for an age defined by emergence.

Opening the Circle: What's Ahead

We are living through a collapse that holds the seed of renewal. What looks like a breakdown is, in truth, a Renaissance in disguise.

As in every great turning, it will be the creatives—the Level 7 leaders—who imagine the new order into being. Yet before reordering comes disorder. Before rebirth, the breakdown.

In the next chapter, we will examine why the old operating system of leadership is failing, how its glitches manifest in our organizations and in our bodies, and why facing that failure is the doorway to renewal.

The future is not something coming *at* us.

It is moving *through* us.

The work of leadership is to become the vessel through which emergence itself can flow.

CHAPTER 2

When the Operating System Fails

"We do not notice the wear of the ship until the hull begins to creak under the waves." —LAO TZU *(adapted)*

Leadership doesn't usually unravel because of a bad plan. The real problem is deeper. It first appears as subtle signs of overload felt in the body, like early warning lights flashing quietly in the background, well before the mind can pinpoint what is wrong.

At first, everything appears stable: green lights, road maps clear, team confident. But beneath the polished surface, the pattern cracks. An angry customer conversation escalates, a regulator messages about an early inspection, the model wobbles, the board demands a pivot. Outwardly, everything remains calm, while the deeper system creaks and groans.

The organization keeps moving, but the leader's internal operating system—their mental and emotional wiring—begins to glitch. It's as if a computer tries to run too many programs at once and starts slowing down or freezing. This is what is happening in the human nervous system.

The body is first to signal: chest tightness, shallow breathing, or a feeling of the air growing thin. Words come out, but the leader's presence is fading. The organization still runs, but the pilot (meaning the leader) is no longer fully in control of the cockpit.

When the leader's dashboard blinks red, the organization's learning slows. The interface looks normal, but the system is stuck. I saw this all the time in Army Ranger School, when a Ranger candidate had met his limit. Tasks are done, but adaptation stalls. The team unconsciously tunes into the leader's anxiety, contracting collective creativity.

The code we run—our collective operating system—was written for a world that moved at the rhythm of seasons, not the tachycardia of notifications today.

Industrial-era management valued predictability over presence. That logic made sense when markets moved at a human tempo, information gaps softened risk, and strategies unfolded over years rather than weeks.

Today, we find ourselves navigating a multi-vector landscape, where change arrives from every direction at once.

- Generative AI reshapes industries monthly, sometimes weekly.
- Global supply networks respond in milliseconds.
- Social narratives mutate at network speed.

Exponential signals now collide with a nervous system that still expects change to happen slowly, not in rapid bursts. If we don't pause and reset, our minds fall back on old habits: We narrow our attention, react with stress, and stop learning, just like a computer enters safe mode and turns off nonessential functions to avoid crashing. It was helpful during the hunter-gatherer period. Not helpful in the age of AI.

Even the best strategy can't rescue an organization if its physiology lags behind change. The operating system fails before the strategy starts.

The Science of Overload

This isn't a personal failing; it's ancient biology at work.

Under threats like reputational risk, time pressure, ambiguity or overload, the amygdala fires milliseconds before the thinking cortex can respond.[9]

And this impairs the very executive functions leaders rely on most—working memory, inhibitory control, and cognitive flexibility.[10]

How it plays out in the human operating system:

1. **Alarm:** The amygdala fires before conscious reasoning.
2. **Shift:** Fight (push harder), flight (avoid or deflect), or freeze (comply or numb) is chosen.
3. **Narrowing:** Creative capacity collapses; time horizons shrink.
4. **Contagion:** The leader's state becomes the team's through micro expressions and mirroring.

Ironically, the very capacities we need most—creativity and perspective—are the first to vanish when the system is under threat.

State shapes story. The body decides safety before the mind can catch up. That's why leaders recognize the "rainbow-wheel" moment, not just as a digital freeze, but as a full-body stall. The body locks up first; thought lags behind.

Why It Matters to Founders and Executives

As a founder piloting a venture-backed rocket or an executive steering a billion-dollar division, you know this isn't theory. You've experienced the slow-burn exhaustion of firefights and decision fatigue—terrain that can challenge even elite teams.

When the nervous system locks into survival mode, learning drops offline. Innovation demands exploration, but the body is broadcasting only for safety. More market opportunities close due to silent leadership collapse than to flawed ideas. But most business books do not focus on this most foundational element.

Military Glimpse: Fire, Freeze, and the Physics of Stress

Elite military training offers a vivid parallel, and one that I know well from my time in the army.

S. L. A. Marshall claimed that only 15% to 25% of US infantry fired their weapons in some World War II battles.[11] Later scholars debated the numbers,[12] but the freeze response itself is undisputed.

Under threat, as defined by being fired upon—*literally* being shot at in combat environments—humans often freeze; it's a defense developed during evolution. Modern militaries counter this with stress inoculation, like the Malvesti Obstacle Course at Army Ranger School, which includes live-fire drills, decision-making after days without food or sleep, and chaos rehearsals.

The leadership lesson is clear: Under maximum stress, people don't default to skilled action but to habits or paralysis, just as a computer under strain switches to basic functions. Unless we train differently to show up with a different state of mind, our inner operating system will always prefer survival over noticing what's happening in real time.

Business Translation: The Hidden Cost of Freeze

Your first product outage isn't a battlefield, but your nervous system cannot distinguish between a company crisis and actual danger. In both, the body reacts the same way.

When executives lack state agility—detect → name → downshift—organizations display a civilian version of battlefield freeze:

- Contrarian ideas dry up.
- Decisions stall while teams "wait for more data."
- Everyone mirrors the leader's rising cortisol.

Biology will always outpace ideology. The antidote is to design your leadership and organization for biology, not just belief.

Case Studies in Operating-System Overload

The following case studies translate the science of overload into lived reality. Each illustrates how modern organizations confront the same invisible failure point: when biological limits collide with exponential complexity. In each scenario, what looked like a systems or strategy breakdown was, in fact, a human one: the moment the leader's operating system overheated and the collective intelligence froze. Yet as these examples reveal, recovery begins not with a new plan, but with a physiological reset: simple, structured pauses that restore coherence, clarity, and collective flow.

KRAFTWERKE GRÜN—WHEN THE SYSTEM FREEZES FROM THE INSIDE

In early 2025, *Harvard Business Review* profiled Kraftwerke Grün, a German renewable energy firm that had just emerged from a near bankruptcy and was undergoing rapid transformation. The board brought in a new CEO, Alex Reinhardt, to lead the turnaround. A respected strategist with strong credentials, Reinhardt approached the role with intensity—working long hours, absorbing multiple priorities, and pushing hard through structural resistance.

Then he collapsed.

Reinhardt fainted in his office, hit his head, and was rushed to the hospital. The diagnosis: exhaustion, dehydration, and burnout. A red-alert moment. His internal operating system had crashed. The board, shocked, paused the transformation effort to confront a difficult question: Can a company move faster than its leadership nervous system can handle?

What followed was a collective reckoning. While the company's operations had kept pace with demand, the executive bandwidth—physiological and emotional—had degraded. Teams reported hesitation, narrowed focus, and vanishing creativity. Decisions slowed. Momentum drained.

The board had assumed that Reinhardt's breakdown was a personal issue. It wasn't. It was a system-level signal.

The organization, like its leader, had slipped into "safe mode"—a kind of organizational freeze. The problem wasn't the strategy; it was the state.

Harvard Business Review framed it this way: In high-pressure environments, biology outpaces ideology.[13] A plan can be sound, but the organism executing it must be sounder. Leadership can no longer be separated from physiology. Boards must now assess not only vision and execution, but coherence, executive presence, recovery capacity, and nervous system resilience.

Reinhardt's collapse became a turning point. The company introduced new cadence protocols, recovery windows between strategic sprints, and team-wide awareness training rooted in physiology. This wasn't a wellness initiative; it was an operating system reboot.

The insight is clear: The body fails before the strategy does. And in today's business environment, resilience begins not with speed, but with state.

SHOPIFY'S "RED FRIDAY" RESET

During the 2022 holiday rush, Shopify faced a triple shock: a seventeen-hour outage of its payments partner, a zero-day vulnerability, and a TikTok-driven traffic surge.

The first all-hands ran long and loud. Slack pings multiplied while proposals thinned. Engineers hesitated to deploy fixes without sign-off.

COO Kaz Nejatian noticed the drift into sympathetic mobilization, a state of high arousal and low creativity.[14] He called a ten-minute pause and initiated a coherence stack: two minutes of breathing followed by a single question: "What is reversible in the next ninety minutes?"

Teams self-organized around that constraint. Within three hours, a payment workaround was launched, a security patch deployed, and marketing reframed the outage as a limited-edition "Red Friday" sale that boosted conversions. **CEO** Tobi Lütke **has since described moments like this as evidence that resilience at Shopify is fundamentally a human systems problem before it is a technical one.**[15]

Across industries, the pattern is familiar. First, a series of shocks hit, then physiology takes over: Attention narrows, creativity drops, and stress hormones spike. Next, the leader's state ripples outward, spreading stress so that it becomes the organization's default mode. It's only when someone introduces a reset—like a pause, breath, or check-in—that the group regains its sense of connection, making innovation possible again.

Practical Mitigation: From Overload to Coherence

In a crisis, the decisive factor is rarely a brilliant strategy deck. It's the state of the leader and the team. The real question is how to embed coherence into daily practice so stability becomes structure rather than just reaction.

Personal Physiology: Breath as Bandwidth

Neuroscience confirms what contemplative traditions have long known: The fastest way to shift state is through the breath. Roughly 80% of vagus nerve fibers carry signals from the body to the brain, offering a direct channel to calm the autonomic system.[16]

Consider the following tips for mindset shifts through the breath.

- **Exhale-dominant breathing:** Inhale for four seconds, then exhale for six to eight. The elongated exhale engages the vagal brake, slowing heart rate and widening perception.[17]
- **Box + extend:** Inhale for four seconds, hold for four, exhale for six, hold for two. This builds CO_2 tolerance and nervous-system flexibility.
- **Micro pauses:** Insert sixty-second breath checks between calendar blocks. A silent hourly alarm prevents urgency from accumulating.

Team-Level Resets

While individual self-regulation is vital, a team's effectiveness depends on its ability to reach a shared, coherent state. Social neuroscience shows that people frequently **unconsciously synchronize bodily functions**, such as heart rate and breathing, when they share an experience or pay attention to the same stimulus. Even something as simple as listening attentively to a story can align heart-rate patterns among listeners. This physiological synchrony is driven by engagement and shared cognitive processing, not just emotional connection, and it reflects how deeply our bodies respond together during coordinated experiences.

Here are several practical techniques for helping teams reset and regain coherence under stress:

- **Coherence huddles:** Begin important meetings with two minutes of guided breathing. This pause invites physiological alignment and helps "bring the room online" by anchoring attention and calming the nervous system.
- **Decision gates:** Before taking irreversible actions, run a quick checkpoint by asking yourself these questions:
    1. "Do we have sufficient data?"
    2. "Are the consequences reversible?"
    3. "Is our collective state coherent?"

If two or more answers are "No," implement a twelve-hour pause to reassess.

- **Color-code check-ins:** Start check-ins by having each member share their state using a simple scale—**green**, **yellow**, or **red**— with one sentence of context. This builds emotional awareness and surface-level alignment.

- **Edge-listening rounds:** Invite contributions, starting with the quietest voices in the room. Research on psychological safety shows that creating space for all perspectives is one of the strongest predictors of team innovation and shared understanding.

Closing Reflection

Level 7 leadership isn't about eliminating stress. It's about mastering the state at the center of complexity. Breath becomes bandwidth. Pause becomes performance.

The next chapter explores how this inner architecture links to the outer act of decision-making, where sensing, coherence, and decisive action converge. For founders and executives navigating exponential change that engulfs us today, the invitation is simple: Design your organization with the same care you give your business strategy and treat physiology as core infrastructure. Only then can you lead at the true velocity of the human+machine era.

CHAPTER 3

Beyond Servant Leadership

"Discontent is the first necessity of progress."—THOMAS EDISON

"Innovation distinguishes between a leader and a follower."—STEVE JOBS

———————

The compass, the map, and the landscape have all changed. Leadership is now a dynamic process, navigating a landscape defined by relentless and accelerating change. The challenge is to sharpen our inner senses to adapt in real time.

The era of hierarchical leadership is fading, replaced by a shifting frontier. The real task is to sense and respond to change as it happens, embracing what is emerging, not resisting it.

A World of Concurrent Breakthroughs

Consider a single day in 2025:

- **AI and generative models:** Large-language models double in capability every six months, and 80% of Fortune 500 firms report pilot deployments across at least three core business functions.[18]

- **Biotechnology:** CRISPR-based therapies clear Phase III trials for sickle-cell disease while synthetic-biology start-ups attract a record $20 billion in venture funding.[19]
- **Quantum computing:** IBM and Google each announces milestone demonstrations of error-corrected qubits, compressing problems once thought decades away into the near term.

These are not isolated breakthroughs but *converging waves* amplifying one another. The World Economic Forum reports a fivefold surge in global patent filings across AI, quantum, and biotech in ten years. Renowned economist, researcher, and professor Erik Brynjolfsson calls this pace "super-exponential." It is so steep that it transforms both forecasts and mental models.[20]

Cognitive Whiplash for Leaders

The impact that humans are feeling in this era is nothing short of profound. When "future shock" events begin to stack—AI and automation disruptions, geopolitical or technological choke points, regulatory upheavals, radical shifts in consumer behavior, or large-scale digital infrastructure failures—leaders are thrust into states of cognitive overload.

Three-time Pulitzer Prize-winning journalist Thomas Friedman aptly describes this as "the age of acceleration, where our capacity to adapt is tested daily."[21] I know this feeling firsthand. I've been experiencing it, consciously, since at least 2019, when I began building in AI. The technology landscape was shifting and evolving so rapidly that as soon as I felt like I knew the right path forward, the business landscape would radically accelerate—like with ChatGPT's launch in 2022.

According to research from the American Psychological Association, chronic exposure to unpredictable change elevates cortisol levels and impairs working memory.[22] For many executives, this is today's psychological terrain: navigating complexity under the weight of decision fatigue and neural strain.

Yet within this volatility lies an unexpected opportunity. For those who meet the moment with curiosity rather than resistance, disorientation can quickly give way to exhilaration. These leaders recognize that they are operating in a rapidly emerging planetary nervous system—an interconnected digital-intentional landscape—where aligning thought and action can happen at the speed of now.

The Executive's Dilemma

If you are leading today, you know the tension: The old playbook lags behind the tempo of the new world. You have honored the rules; secured the right degrees and certifications; built trust with your team, vendors, and clients; and shaped organizations. Yet the social contract that once promised meaning in exchange for loyalty is dissolving underfoot. The old agreement—"Do these things, and you will be happy and successful"—is no longer there. A friend of mine, Kate Allinson, calls this the "messy middle." This middle includes executives who have the title and the material things but are lost without feeling connected to a higher purpose or a framework for moving forward.

Generational Crosscurrents

- Baby boomers valued stability and a clear career path. They aimed to climb the ladder and retire with security, viewing organizational loyalty and predictability as keys to success.
- Gen X, shaped by economic downturns and frequent layoffs, learned to be resilient and adaptable, viewing career security as uncertain and prizing independence out of necessity.
- Millennials seek purpose in their work, prioritizing meaning over status. However, as they confront high workplace expectations, over 40% now report chronic stress, feeling the tension between aspiration and burnout.[23]
- Gen Z, the first fully digital generation, prioritizes authenticity, flexibility, and mental health above traditional authority. They value openness and work-life balance, often putting these before hierarchy or rigid advancement structures.[24]

Deloitte's 2024 *Millennial & Gen Z Survey* found that 40% would leave a higher-paying job if the work lacked meaning, and 60% ranked work-life balance above advancement.[25] Gallup adds that six in ten Gen Z employees refuse roles requiring full-time office presence.[26] They no longer want to follow the map; they want to co-create it.

Three Faces of the New Reality

- **Alex, the Gen X COO:** Decades of Six Sigma discipline meet weekly AI pivots, producing constant decision fatigue.
- **Maya, the millennial VP:** Purpose-driven but drained by endless status meetings, she eyes a start-up for autonomy and impact.
- **Jordan, the Gen Z engineer:** A coding prodigy who values boundaries, he expects psychological safety and visible integrity, or he exits.

These stories show a new pattern: Once-valued instincts, like discipline and control, now risk becoming constraints as inherited habits diverge from new realities.

I have felt this dynamic tension between the old ways and the new ways of being and leading in my own experience. As a member of the Gen X generation, a West Point engineer, and a financial services entrepreneur turned tech builder, it has often left me feeling unstable, fatigued, and unsure as a leader.

A Personal Glitch: West Point Rigor Meets AI Tempo

When I became CEO of TIFIN in 2019, the shift from traditional finance to AI-driven fintech was abrupt. Annual plans became weekly sprints in a world of accelerating technology on all fronts. Speed was a constant at TIFIN—it was the environment.

As I mentioned in Chapter 1, we decided early to pursue innovation on multiple fronts simultaneously. But my human operating system was not prepared for the speed, ambiguity, and constant context switching. We were developing multiple products in real time—Magnifi, Positivly, and Give were just a few of the platforms—while simultaneously raising capital and building strategic partnerships with J.P. Morgan, among others.

I had been a founder before, and I was familiar with the chaos of early-stage life. But this time, it was decidedly different: It was AI driven and fast. I was being pulled into machine-level precision and speed.

In most of the Friday OKR (Objectives and Key Results) meetings, I could smell ammonia wafting up from my body, a familiar scent that I recognized from the stresses of Army Ranger School and West Point. It was a clear sign that my nervous system was at the limit and my body was beginning to burn muscle in a fight-or-flight state. And it was not just me. The room was filled with this smell, and everyone was holding their breath. They, too, had reached their growth edge.

The lessons that had gotten them into the room—leaders building the next phase of AI in fintech—were failing them in real time, and I was "leading" the way.

When Rigor Becomes a Liability

The US Army's five-paragraph Operations Order—Situation, Mission, Execution, Support, Command—builds confidence before chaos. Yet as any Ranger knows, once the first round fires, the plan melts.

Today's markets and companies echo that volatility. Success is less about perfect plans and more about adaptive response. The rigor that once brought order can now harden into rigidity. The new discipline is improvisation, meeting the unknown with presence and agility.

Servant Leadership: Moral but Misaligned

Robert Greenleaf's 1970 essay "The Servant as Leader" inspired generations to serve first and lead second. Companies like Starbucks and Southwest Airlines credited servant-leadership principles for improved trust and retention, and meta-analyses confirm strong links between engagement and commitment.[27]

Yet good intentions, on their own, are no longer enough to keep pace with the rate of change. Greenleaf's model was born from large, stable organizations like AT&T, where Robert worked in the early part of the last century. At that time, attention and energy invested in an individual could pay dividends over long periods of time.

This is a new era.

When Service Slows the System

A 2020 *Harvard Business Review* survey of three hundred high-tech firms found that "pure" servant-leadership cultures underperformed peers by up to 20% on speed to market and innovation.[28] Consensus, while compassionate, struggles under exponential load. Worse, servant leadership can mask hierarchy—the benevolent "father figure" serving from above rather than among.

Comparing Leadership Models

Servant (Greenleaf)	Empathy, trust, psychological safety	Slower decisions; over-consensus
Transformational (Burns)	Inspiring vision; intrinsic motivation	Charisma dependence
Adaptive (Heifetz)	Learning loops; experimentation	Ambiguity tolerance required
Level 7 (Proposed)	Energy and intuition; collective coherence	Requires state mastery

Servant leadership moved us beyond command and control. But as complexity compounds, the call is to evolve again—to sense and shape change at the speed at which it arrives.

Why Servant Leadership Can't Carry Us Forward

Robert Greenleaf's insight remains morally brilliant. Yet, as Brené Brown writes, "Strong ground is forged when we learn to stand in tension without demanding immediate resolution."[29]

Consensus and deliberation—virtues in stability—become liabilities in cascade. Leaders must hold paradox: speed and safety, authority and humility, data and intuition. Brown warns, "When we mistake comfort for clarity, we abandon the very values we intend to protect."[30]

Harvard's longitudinal study of 1,200 managers put it bluntly: *Trust without speed is a warm blanket in a burning building.*[31] Level 7 leadership keeps the moral center of service but adds the courage to move at the velocity of change.

Evidence from Harvard, Wharton, and the Frontier

A 2023 Wharton study of 260 global firms found that distributed-leadership organizations outperformed hierarchies by 34% in innovation speed and 28% in time to market.[32]

Shopify begins meetings with ninety-second pulse checks and empowers teams to ship code the same day a signal appears.

Bayer's Pharmaceuticals division restructured around agile pods during COVID-19, pushing decision-making down to cross-functional teams. Scientists no longer waited for top-down approval to move. Speed increased, silos thinned, and innovation flowed.[33]

Atlassian's open Team Playbook decentralizes authority and trust, fueling enduring growth.

Resilience and speed are born from distributed coherence, not from command. The future belongs to those who can weave alignment across the system, not just direct it from above.

Service from the Center

> *"True service is not giving up yourself; it's giving from your center."*
> —RAM DASS

True service begins where self-sacrifice leaves off. Leadership has often romanticized the emptying of self for others, but emptiness without connection only leads to depletion. Ram Dass flipped the script: Real service is not about running on empty, but about giving from a place of inner abundance.

When a leader serves from the center, action arises from coherence rather than compliance. They are not trying to please or rescue; they are expressing wholeness. Neuroscience confirms it: When heart rhythm, breath, and brain synchronize, leaders emit steadier electromagnetic fields that entrain their teams, enhancing trust and creativity.[34] More on this in Chapter 11.

Across traditions, the pattern is the same:

- **Buddhism:** The Bodhisattva serving through presence
- **Taoism:** *Wu wei*, or effortless action in harmony with flow
- **Indigenous and Druidic paths:** *Ayni*, or sacred reciprocity with life itself.

Leadership at this level is not about depletion, but transmission. The leader's grounded presence becomes the field that organizes others. In practice, the CEO settles a room before a decision, the founder breathes before speaking, and the manager allows wisdom to surface before acting.

To serve from the center is to become **stability in motion**, the still point in a spinning world. Level 7 leaders understand that presence is power. Their energy does not scatter; it steadies. Service is not martyrdom, but mastery. From this grounded place, action is both swift and compassionate.

This is the next evolution: not serving others from depletion, but serving the whole from coherence.

Rediscovering Fast Intelligence

Modern leadership has worshipped slow logic—analysis, metrics, dashboards—while the world now moves faster than thought. The spreadsheet is always a step behind the signal.

Level 7 leadership reclaims what ancient leaders understood: The body itself is an instrument of knowing. Intuition is not mysticism; it is biology tuned for complexity.

Neuroscience shows that intuitive insight arises when the prefrontal cortex, limbic system, and gut-brain axis synchronize milliseconds before conscious thought.[35] What feels like a "gut sense" is the nervous system running predictive simulations faster than language can name them.

When a leader's physiology is coherent—heart, breath, and brain in resonance—this fast intelligence comes online. Fragmented by stress, it vanishes beneath the noise.

Ram Dass called it "service from the center"; science calls it decision-making from coherence. Level 7 leaders pause not to slow down, but to tune up and align their inner instrument with the field around them. The pause is not inaction; it is the precision of presence.

From that stillness, intuition rises like a sonar ping from the deep, guiding motion before data arrives. Logic verifies; intuition initiates.

The future will not be led by those who think the fastest, but by those who sense the earliest—leaders who feel the tremor before the trend. Intuition is not the opposite of intelligence; it *is intelligence, accelerated.*

Reflective Practices for the Level 7 Leader

- **Center before you serve:** Begin each day with three slow exhale-dominant breaths. Ask, "From what state am I about to lead?" Service from depletion breeds distortion; service from the center creates coherence.
- **Keep an intuition journal:** Record one moment each day when you knew before you could explain. Note how it felt in your body, what signals preceded it, and what outcome followed. Patterns will teach you your intuitive language.
- **Pause with a ninety-second reset:** Before major meetings, pause for ninety seconds of collective silence or slow breathing. This shifts group physiology toward coherence, creating clarity faster than another slide deck.
- **Practice edge listening:** Once a week, invite a perspective from outside your comfort zone—an intern, a customer, an AI assistant— and listen for the faint signals of what's emerging.
- **Calibrate in nature:** Step outside weekly with no agenda. Let the rhythm of wind or water retune your nervous system. Remember: Coherence with nature precedes coherence in teams.
- **Perform an energy audit:** At week's end, map what activities expanded or drained your energy. Vitality data is as real as financial data. Lead from what gives life, not what drains you.

Each practice is a doorway back to coherence—an invitation to lead from the living intelligence within.

From Inner Shift to Organizational Design

The journey beyond servant leadership is a threshold into deeper growth. We have mapped the shift from linear to multi-vector leadership, explored why consensus alone cannot keep pace, and seen how sovereign, intuitive leaders hold paradox, anchored in strong ground, even as they move at the speed of emergence.

Inner mastery is only a step on the path. The next step is to translate that agility into outer architecture: culture, structure, and rhythms that can adapt as fluidly as the leader. In the next chapter, Level 7 leadership moves from the personal to the systemic, from the sovereign intuitive leader to the learning organization.

CHAPTER 4

A New Renaissance—The Call for Creativity

"They didn't just play the game better. They reimagined how the game could be played."—ANDY WALSHE, *Co-Founder of Liminal Collective*

———————

Sometimes, history seems to pause, as if the world is holding its breath. In these pauses, we can sense new opportunities quietly gathering beneath the surface, waiting to emerge.

During these times, old ways of thinking fade, and it feels like our understanding of reality is about to change. We are now together, right now, at that moment of expectation and readiness for change.

A few reasons why:

- The volume of scientific knowledge now doubles every decade, accelerating the tempo of discovery.
- Generative AI models, including machines that write code for machines, reinvent their own playbooks with each passing quarter,

learning at a pace that outstrips our old maps.

- Cultural memes now orbit the globe in minutes, weaving new patterns of meaning at the speed of light.

It feels like we are at the edge of what is familiar, noticing a calm surface while powerful changes, though invisible, are quietly reshaping our world. Real transformation often starts in ways we can't immediately *think* with our brains. It occurs in the realms of ideas and imagination before emerging into the known world. The emergence can be felt in the stillness and quiet before being heard or thought.

The Florentines of the fifteenth century recognized this sensation, even if they could not yet name it. They felt the old scaffolding of guilds and dogma straining to contain a new surge of human imagination.

Now our supporting structures are digital, built from code rather than stone. But history repeats: Changes now happen instantly. This is not just digital transformation; it is a fast shift in how people imagine, make, and connect ideas.

Leaders who hold tightly to control will find their strategies overtaken, not by a single disruption, but by a rising tide of possibilities that refuse to be contained. The real invitation is to ride the wave, to become co-creators at the living edge where emergence happens, and to get comfortable and confident at this edge.

Echo of the First Renaissance

The original Renaissance was more than artistic genius; it was a *rewiring of civilization's operating system.* Gutenberg's press (c. 1440) shattered the church's information monopoly.[36] The Medici family became the early venture capitalists, financially backing initiatives at the edge of imagination. Humanism, articulated by Pico della Mirandola and Erasmus, placed humanity back in the role of creator. Leonardo da Vinci's sketches of flying machines and hydraulic pumps captured a mind that saw centuries ahead.[37]

Parallels Are Unmistakable

PRINTING PRESS ⇄ INTERNET AND AI

Gutenberg shattered the bottleneck of knowledge; AI is doing the same. Yet while Gutenberg accelerated the *distribution* of established knowledge, AI accelerates the *creation* of new insights. And, increasingly, it *actions* them.

FLORENTINE GUILDS ⇄ OPEN-SOURCE NETWORKS

Apprenticeship once meant loyalty to a single master; now it comes from whoever holds the next piece of knowledge you need on your journey—a global, ever-shifting constellation of mentors on platforms like YouTube, Reddit, and MasterClass.

AGE OF EXPLORATION ⇄ MAPPING THE QUANTUM AND HUMAN POTENTIAL

Explorers once mapped geography; today, explorers chart new terrains of thought, possibility, and consciousness. The edge of understanding was once marked on physical maps—"Here be dragons." Now it lies within the unbounded frontier of the human mind and spirit.

The lesson endures: Invest in the commons, honor beauty and utility equally, and dwell in the *liminal zone*, where boundaries blur and new worlds gestate—the space of being "in between."

Technology as Canvas

If the first Renaissance was animated by the press and the patron. This next turning is powered by code and computation. AI is no longer just a tool for efficiency; it is becoming a co-creator at the edge of our collective imagination.

Designers now collaborate with diffusion models to conjure structures that echo the intelligence of coral reefs. Biologists invite algorithms to hypothesize new proteins in days, not decades. Synthetic biologists approach DNA as living code, a language to be composed. Space entrepreneurs are making orbit as accessible as the open sea.

Open AI platforms, maker communities, and decentralized finance ecosystems are less like machines and more like living ecologies—complex, adaptive, and always in motion. These systems resist top-down control, thrive on diversity, and flourish through open collaboration. They are not instruments to command, but living systems to steward and cultivate.

Within these living systems, creativity is not an optional extra; it is a core survival skill. Those who cling to control are outpaced by those who can sense, adapt, and co-create with the unknown. Influence now accrues to those who cultivate emergence, not those who enforce predictability. The leaders who matter most are not gatekeepers, but gardeners who tend the soil where new patterns and possibilities can take root.

Reality itself becomes our shared canvas, open to the possibilities we can imagine and shape together.

Creatives as the Architects of Evolution

The creatives consistently lead humanity's next evolution. They reimagine governments, schools, religions, and businesses because they see new ways of being—more fluid, more adaptive, more alive than what came before.

They are the dreamers who dream civilizations into being, the imaginal architects of each new era. Their visions become the operating systems of the future—the ideas, rituals, and enterprises that move humanity into its next chapter.

Every major leap—from Florence to Silicon Valley, from the Enlightenment to the Information Age—began not with management plans, but with imagination daring enough to question what others took for granted. The creative leader's work is to reveal the invisible architectures that shape our world, pausing, listening, attuning, and creating the context for the new ideas to be revealed.

The Neuroscience of Creativity: From Default Mode to Flow

To lead now is to recognize creativity not as magic, but as a living process within the brain's own dynamics.

Brain-imaging studies show that creative insight emerges when two systems, the default-mode network (imagination and memory) and the executive-control network (focus and evaluation), enter rhythmic dialogue.[38] During ideation, alpha and theta waves synchronize across hemispheres, enabling the brain to generate and assess ideas almost simultaneously. This is the flow structure. Mihaly Csikszentmihalyi described it as merging action and awareness.[39] In this state, time slows, self-doubt fades, and pattern recognition increases. It is when our minds work most smoothly.

A McKinsey study found that executives in flow are five times more productive.[40] In flow, they act like a river: gentle, powerful, and able to self-correct.

Elite Creators and Group Flow

My friend Andy Walshe, co-founder of Liminal Collective, spent years studying the world's top 0.0001% of performers. His conclusion was that they didn't just play the game better; they *reimagined* the game itself.

Michael Jordan turned basketball into art. Tiger Woods transformed golf into a sport. Shaun White built a secret half-pipe in the backcountry—no cameras, no crowd—to explore possibilities without pressure. Their edge wasn't mechanics; it was *imagination.*

Walshe's research revealed that when these athletes entered flow, neural noise dropped, dopamine and anandamide surged, and the boundary between self and system dissolved.

Flow in Special Operations: A Field Parable

Elite Special Operations teams learn to enter non-ordinary states to improve team unity. They use sensory deprivation, breath control, and neurofeedback to quiet the mind and react quickly. In this state, the team acts as one unit, making decisions faster than conscious thought. I first learned about this at Army Ranger School and later from my partner, Jurgen Heitmann, co-founder of Liminal Collective, who spent twenty-seven years as a navy special warfare officer with the SEALs.

This same phenomenon now informs innovation teams. While I was at Liminal, we had clients from some of the most innovative companies in the world, seeking to apply and train in these same principles. When physiological boundaries soften, collective intelligence amplifies, and teaming, trust, and communication increase.[41]

The Shadow of the Renaissance: When Control Masquerades as Creation

Even with expanded intelligence, every Renaissance casts a shadow. The same technologies that expand imagination can also compress it. Algorithmic feeds narrow perspective. AI-generated content risks a culture of replication rather than revelation.

Philosopher Hannah Arendt warned that "the banality of evil" arises from thoughtlessness—the refusal to imagine otherwise. When leaders optimize solely for efficiency, they trade creativity for control. Shoshana Zuboff calls this the "age of surveillance capitalism," where data replaces dialogue and prediction replaces participation.[42]

The antidote is *presence*. Creative leadership means continually rehumanizing technology, making sure that algorithms serve imagination rather than the reverse. The leader's presence creates the stability for new ideas to flow.

Flow Teams and Collective Creativity

At Liminal Collective and earlier at TIFIN, I observed teams entering what Steven Kotler termed "shared ecstasis." Breaths synchronized, agendas faded, and solutions emerged from beyond individual intellect.[43]

Research from MIT's Human Dynamics Lab confirms that collective intelligence correlates not with IQ averages but with equal turn-taking and emotional attunement.[44] Heart-rate monitors show that high-performing teams come into rhythmic coherence within minutes of alignment.

The pattern repeats at every scale: from individuals to teams, from organizations to societies. As coherence grows, creativity multiplies.

The Physics of Emergence: Order → Disorder → Reorder

Belgian physical chemist and Nobel Laureate Ilya Prigogine explained that some systems become more ordered through instability.[45] Life grows at the edge of chaos.

Leadership in the human+machine era follows this same rhythm: Order gives way to disorder, which then reorganizes into a new pattern. Creativity asks us to stand in the uncertainty long enough for a new coherence to emerge.

This is the alchemy of advanced leadership: holding enough heat for transformation without so much that the vessel is lost.

Case Lens: Generative Design and Emergent Order

Generative design allows AI to explore thousands of permutations in minutes, optimizing for strength, cost, and beauty. Airbus used it to reinvent an A320 partition modeled after bone tissue, 45% lighter yet stronger than the original. Architects design buildings that breathe with light and wind; Singapore planners use algorithms to maximize community and green space.

Beyond structures, generative design informs fashion, furniture, and medicine. Nike's Flyprint uppers and AI-driven molecular discovery illustrate a new covenant between human and machine: imagination as collaboration.

Leadership itself becomes a form of generative design: setting intention, welcoming surprise, and curating the conditions for emergence.

Reflective Practices: The Creative Alchemy

If leadership is a generative art, then reflection is its studio practice. What follows are not habits but strategic frameworks, deliberate practices designed to activate the creative state where imagination, intuition, and innovation converge. With practice, what is at first state becomes trait.

- **State switch:** Notice the instant before stress closes your system. Exhale three times, drop your shoulders, and soften your gaze. You've reopened the channel of imagination.
- **Constraint as catalyst:** Once a week, impose a creative limit: ten minutes, three slides, one sentence. This invites elegance through restriction.
- **Embodied flow:** Walk, run, or dance until thought loosens. The body thinks faster than the mind.[46]
- **Shadow dialogue:** Write a letter to the fear you avoid. Ask what it protects. Often, the shadow guards your next gift.
- **Co-creation circle:** Gather a small team. Set a shared intention. No slides. Just story, silence, and sensing. Notice how ideas emerge from the space between.

- **Beauty as strategy:** Visit a gallery, mountain, or concert each month.

Beauty retunes the nervous system faster than any off-site agenda. Creativity is not just a function; it is a frequency. These practices help tune the instrument of leadership to receive and amplify it.

Final Invocation: The Renaissance Requires Your Whole Self

This age does not simply ask you to manage change. It invites you to *become* the change itself.

Let your body register the yes of a future idea.

Let intuition light the doorway.

Let reason build the scaffolding.

Let your heart signal the timing.

The cathedrals of this age will not be built of stone. They will be built of *coherence*, a deep understanding, and alignment of purpose, values, strategy, and actions. Leaders and teams will be so attuned that imagination moves through them as freely as electricity through a circuit.

Step forward not just with your skills, but also with your spirit.

The Renaissance never begins in boardrooms or parliaments. It starts in the human spirit, in the willingness to breathe into the unknown and trust that what lies beyond uncertainty is not chaos, but creation itself.

CHAPTER 5

The Myth of the Solo Leader

From Heroic Independence to Collective Intelligence

"The hero's journey always ends where it began . . . but with the leader no longer at the center of the story." —JOSEPH CAMPBELL

The Hero Leader Illusion

The solitary hero is a pattern etched deep into the Western psyche. From Achilles on the plains of Troy to Steve Jobs on a darkened stage, we orbit the gravitational pull of the lone visionary, one who seems to bend reality through force of will. But this chapter argues that the myth of the solo leader, so familiar and pervasive, limits what leadership can be. American writer, mythologist, and lecturer Joseph Campbell mapped this as *the hero's journey:* a universal operating system in which the protagonist departs, faces an ordeal, and returns changed.[47]

But what if this myth is only one lens on the map?

Industrial capitalism took this myth and coded it into its DNA. The Great Man theory, championed by Scottish philosopher Thomas Carlyle, reframed history as a sequence of heroic interventions. Management science followed, with Taylor's scientific management recasting organizations as machines, workers as interchangeable parts, and the leader as the sole architect. The result was a system wired for control, with the myth of indispensability at its core.

This mindset built bridges and railroads, but it also rewired our collective nervous system. Leadership became synonymous with dominance, clarity with certainty, and safety with hierarchy. The cost was a narrowing of what leadership could be.

As exponential technology rewires every feedback loop on the planet, a new chapter beckons. Where the lone hero once stabilized, we are now invited to gather, to build something nobler and more resilient.

Complexity now outpaces any single mind. Algorithms move markets in microseconds. Shifting climate systems ripple across continents. Culture evolves at the speed of networks. In this new terrain, heroic control breeds fragility instead of resilience.

What emerges instead is collective coherence, with the leader carefully sensing what is emerging: intelligence distributed through relationship, trust, and shared sensing. The hero archetype doesn't vanish; it dissolves into the field, shifting from commander to catalyst. This is the edge where Level 7 leadership begins.

From Industrial Icons to Networked Systems

The twentieth century celebrated a pantheon of singular geniuses: Ford, Welch, Jobs, Bezos, Musk. Their stories, often retold as modern legends, portray them as solitary visionaries. Yet each success was built on vast, vibrant webs of collaboration: engineers, designers, financiers, adopters, and critics, all sharpening vision through creative friction.

Henry Ford's moving assembly line drew on Chicago slaughterhouses' disassembly techniques and was perfected by anonymous machinists who solved local bottlenecks.[48] Jack Welch's vaunted GE boundaryless organization owed its breakthroughs to thousands of Six Sigma teams. Steve

Jobs's reality-distortion field worked only because Jony Ive and Joanna Hoffman could translate vision into craft.[49]

The solo-genius narrative persists because it feeds a deep psychological hunger. In the face of uncertainty, we reach for a central figure, a symbol to anchor our sense of control. Yet often, we trade the comfort of story for the reality of systems at work.

Today, in the networked age, control no longer binds us; it liberates us to create with unprecedented speed. Thriving organizations model themselves after neural networks: adaptable, self-correcting, and alive with possibility. The center isn't retreating in weakness; it is diffusing, empowering brilliance everywhere.

The Speed of Trust

Trust is the essential currency of momentum. It is the felt sense of safety, reliability, and mutual respect that allows people to move decisively together. Human achievement accelerates when trust is present, unlocking purpose and possibility.

When trust is high, decisions move through the network like current through a superconductive wire—no friction, no loss. When trust is low, the circuit jams with fear, hesitation, and politics.

Stephen Covey quantified this dynamic simply: "When trust goes up, speed goes up and cost goes down."[50] Neuroscience confirms why. Oxytocin, the hormone of bonding, lowers threat perception and increases risk tolerance. Dopamine reinforces cooperative action with pleasure feedback. Teams feel faster when trust is present.[51]

Level 7 leaders know that speed without trust is just noise. They treat relational energy as core infrastructure. Every rhythm, meeting cadence, and Slack tone—even body language on a Zoom call—either conducts or resists the current of trust.

The solo-leader myth drains that current, signaling scarcity: power hoarded at the top, information trickling down. On the other hand, cultures of coherence expand trust outward until initiative becomes a shared reflex.

From "I" to "We"

This shift is more than structural; it is existential. Leadership moves from directing outcomes to sensing what wants to emerge. The question evolves. It's not "What do I want to create?" but "What is seeking to come through us?"

This is not to be confused with consensus or other "we" models that dilute solutions through committee. The approach here is seeking information in the pursuit of clarity—not pleasing everyone in the room.

The "I" still matters: Clarity, accountability, and integrity remain anchors. But the "we" is where adaptive intelligence is alive. Moving from "I" to "we" doesn't erase agency; it amplifies it. Collective awareness lets us move with complexity, not against it.

Hidden Networks Behind Hero Myths

History's most celebrated innovators were masters not of solitude, but of orchestration.

Thomas Edison built Menlo Park as the world's first R&D accelerator, a crucible of chemists and machinists iterating thousands of filaments before one glowed steadily. His true invention was the *environment of innovation*.[52]

Henry Ford transformed production not through personal genius but by synthesizing others' ideas into a living system that could learn from its own motion.

Steve Jobs harnessed a small, rebellious tribe (the Macintosh team) bound by aesthetic obsession. Their genius was collective coherence, dozens of minds moving toward elegance in unison.[53]

Charisma may ignite the spark, but only relationships sustain the flame. Level 7 leaders become architects of thriving cultures, intentionally weaving trust and creativity into the fabric of daily life. By their design, workplaces become crucibles of inspiration and the foundation for the emergent.

New Icons of Collaboration

The frontier organizations of the 2020s prove that distributed intelligence outpaces centralized control.

OpenAI advanced from early GPT models to GPT-X through global orchestration: researchers, ethicists, and engineers iterating in public view.[54]

Shopify operationalized Tobi Lütke's "trust batteries" metaphor, where every interaction either charges or drains the invisible energy that makes autonomy safe. Teams with high charge make faster, bolder decisions.[55]

SpaceX treats failure as fuel. Each crash is a data set; each iteration increases the speed of organizational learning. Authority is fluid, distributed to the engineer closest to the telemetry.[56]

In each of these new frontiers, the system becomes the true hero. Trust is the steadfast engine. Curiosity is the common language. What we build together now outshines anything achieved alone.

The Biology of Trust

Trust begins not in philosophy but in physiology.

When two people connect with authentic eye contact, their nervous systems synchronize within seconds. Heart-rate variability, our measure of emotional flexibility, starts to align. This resonance triggers oxytocin release, lowering amygdala activation and allowing the prefrontal cortex to reopen for complex reasoning.[57]

Neuroscientist Paul Zak found that high-trust organizations report 74% less stress and 50% higher productivity than low-trust peers.[58] Yet trust cannot be decreed; it must be *felt*.

Physiological safety precedes psychological safety. The body knows before the mind decides. When a Level 7 leader breathes evenly, listens fully, and responds slowly, they regulate the group's collective vagal tone. Calm becomes contagious.

This is why elite performers practice coherence breathing before high-stakes moments. Navy SEALs use it in pre-mission rituals; heart-rate monitors verify the effect. The vagus nerve, running from the brainstem to the gut, acts like a dimmer switch for anxiety. Lengthening the exhale lowers the internal noise floor, allowing awareness to widen.

Trust, then, is not a soft variable. It is a measurable, trainable, and reproducible biological technology for velocity.

From Command to Coordination:
The Art of Mission Intent

Even the institutions that once epitomized top-down control have evolved toward decentralization and nurturing trust.

In the early 2000s, US Special Operations Forces faced an enemy that moved faster than its command chains. Intelligence gathered in minutes took days to reach decision-makers. By the time orders arrived, the situation had changed. Chaos rewarded adaptability, not hierarchy.

The response was a doctrine called mission command, which combined the clarity of intent with disciplined initiative. Commanders articulated the *why* and *what*; operators decided the *how* in real time.[59]

A young Ranger officer described it this way: "We plan until the first bullet flies, then intent takes over. You trust the people closest to the noise to know what to do."

Before every mission, teams gathered for a *walk-the-board*, a floor map where each member traced movements and identified friction points. Questions surfaced blind spots long before contact. Then came the *premortem*, imagining the mission had failed and listing why.[60] The exercise transformed anxiety into foresight.

Finally, a ritual that corporate leaders would do well to adopt: the *knock-it-off call*. Anyone, regardless of rank, could halt the operation if something felt off. No shame, no delay, just signal.

These practices translate far beyond the battlefield. Swap bullets for market shifts, terrain for data, squads for product teams—and the pattern persists. Clarity without coercion. Authority is distributed through trust.

Imagine a junior member of the go-to-market team calling off a demo for a large enterprise prospect because the product is off and saving a forced restart of a twelve-month sales cycle simply by pushing the demo out a week or two.

Mission command demonstrates that the antidote to chaos is not control but coherence—shared understanding so complete that the group can improvise together without waiting for permission.

Lessons from Living Systems

Nature has been rehearsing distributed leadership for billions of years.

Ant colonies allocate labor without a central planner. Honeybees decide where to build new hives through quorum sensing, which is a democratic waggle dance that balances enthusiasm with caution. Flocks of starlings form vast, pulsating shapes in the sky—murmurations—that shift direction in a fraction of a second. Each bird tracks only a handful of nearby neighbors, yet the entire cloud moves as one coherent body.

These living systems reveal an operating principle older than hierarchy: coherence through connection. Each organism follows simple local rules, attuned to the pulse of the whole. The intelligence that emerges is collective, dynamic, and deeply adaptive.

Physician-ecologist Zach Bush uses this pattern as a metaphor for human potential. In a 2025 reflection, he described murmurations as "the living proof that connection is the blueprint of life," linking the birds' dance to quorum sensing in bacteria, which is the chemical conversation that coordinates ecosystems at the microscopic scale. "Nature is encouraging us each day to remember ourselves as a murmuration, to exist as our blueprint intended, together."[61]

Although the individual ego often misses the point—easily deceived into thinking that going it alone is faster than moving with a team—Bush reminds us that isolation is not our blueprint. The solo leader is as much an illusion as the solitary bird.

Our intelligence—biological, social, spiritual—is fundamentally relational. When we return to that design, leadership becomes coordination, not control; presence, not dominance.

Modern neuroscience echoes this. Synchrony between individuals, measured through brainwave coherence or shared heart-rate variability, correlates with creativity and accuracy in problem-solving.[62] Teams enter physiological resonance. What the mystics called unity consciousness, science now calls *collective flow*.

The Hidden Language of Coherence

In Level 7 organizations, meetings begin not with agendas but with *alignment*. A moment of silence, three steady breaths, or a simple check-in, "Where is your attention right now?" restores physiological harmony before words are spoken.

Research from the HeartMath Institute shows that when one participant enters cardiac coherence, others' heart rhythms tend to synchronize within minutes.[63] The effect is subtle yet measurable. Teams that practice coherence report 40% faster conflict resolution and higher creative throughput.

This is leadership as frequency management. The leader is not the loudest voice, but the clearest signal. Their calm steadies the field, allowing others to sense what is emerging.

Why the Solo Narrative Persists

If collective intelligence is so natural, why do we still cling to the myth of the solo narrative? Because simplicity soothes us. Our minds prefer a single protagonist over a web of interdependence. The media amplify charisma. Shareholders reward the illusion of singular accountability. The hero story puts a human face on uncertainty.

As systems accelerate, that comfort comes at a price. Complexity punishes the closed mind. The next generation of leaders will need to trade admiration for participation, becoming gardeners of coherence instead of warriors of control.

In the human+machine era, the complexity is too great and the speed too fast for another approach.

The Science of Collective Intelligence

A landmark *Science* study identified a *collective intelligence factor*, or *c-factor*, predicting a team's performance across diverse tasks.[64] The driver wasn't average IQ; it was social sensitivity and balanced turn-taking. When participation was equal, the group's accuracy soared.

Scholar of leadership, teaming, and organizational learning Amy Edmondson conducted research into psychological safety that corroborated this: Teams that feel safe to speak up make fewer errors and learn faster.[65] Google's Project

Aristotle later confirmed psychological safety as the top predictor of success across hundreds of teams.[66]

Navy Seals emphasize "Team before Self." Bridgewater Associates, the world's largest hedge fund, emphasizes an "obligation to dissent" as a cultural imperative to ensure that all perspectives are contributed. They credit their long track record to this broad, challenging mode of engaging, which is to say that psychological safety is mostly the permission and expectation to contribute, not that it is easy or doesn't require effort to do so impactfully.

Nature already codes for this. In wolf packs, leadership rotates with the landscape. In coral reefs, diversity sustains resilience. Intelligence grows not from dominance, but from dialogue.

Case Lens: Network Is the Genius

In digital organizations, these principles translate into architecture.

Amazon's "two-pizza teams" maintain autonomy by staying small enough to feed with two pizzas—roughly five to seven members, which is the sweet spot for coordination without bureaucracy.

Wikipedia functions as a living, self-correcting organism: Transparent edits, open discussion pages, and swarm moderation achieve quality control at a global scale.

Liminal Collective, where human-performance scientists, artists, and entrepreneurs collaborate, embodies emergent coherence. Members move between projects fluidly, guided by shared purpose and trust in edge expertise. It is what Andy Walshe calls "designing for aliveness."

In each of these systems, no one holds the whole map. Intelligence circulates through relationships. The leader's work is less about providing direction and more about sustaining connection.

Reflective Practices for the Level 7 Leader

The Circle Check-In

Before strategy, begin with presence. Invite each voice to name one word describing their current state. Listen for the collective mood beneath the words. This harmonizes physiology before intellect engages.

Three-Breath Reset

Between meetings, close your eyes. Inhale through the nose for four counts, exhale for six. Notice your pulse slow. This is not self-care; it is system regulation.

The Premortem

Before launching a major initiative, ask the team to imagine it has failed. Write down every reason. Transform fear into foresight.

Trust Accounting

At the end of each quarter, reflect privately: "Who do I trust more today than three months ago? Who might trust me less?" Repair before planning.

The Murmuration Walk

Take your team outdoors. Walk in silence for ten minutes, matching the pace of those nearest to you. Feel how coordination arises without words. Debrief the sensation of moving as one organism.

These practices are simple yet quietly subversive. They shift leadership from head to field, from strategy to state. Over time, they build what both military and spiritual traditions call unit integrity, which is a felt sense of one heartbeat moving through many bodies.

From Solo to Symphony

The journey beyond the hero myth is not the loss of individuality, but it is fulfillment. The leader who once sought to dominate now learns to conduct. The orchestra expands with humans, machines, and nature each playing a line in the same score.

Level 7 leadership is that score. It tunes human potential to the frequency of emergence. The next great innovation will not come from isolated brilliance, but from relational coherence, which is the same principle that guides flocks, forests, and neural networks.

Zach Bush's invitation echoes here. Remember ourselves as a murmuration, moving through uncertainty with fluid grace. In that remembering, trust becomes the wind beneath collective flight.

The Anatomy of Decision

The myth of the solo leader ends where true leadership begins, which is in the collective field of awareness. We have traced the arc from command to coordination, from hierarchy to coherence, and from fear to trust.

The next challenge is precision: how groups, once coherent, make decisions at the velocity and complexity of the modern world. In the age of AI, decision-making demands not just more data, but deeper discernment, knowing when to move, when to pause, and when to sense the signal beneath the noise.

Chapter 6 explores that frontier: the anatomy of decision, where intuition meets intelligence and the murmuration learns to turn on a dime.

The Anatomy Of A Decision

E ach chapter has added new details to our shared journey.
In Chapter 1, we named the collapse of the old operating system and opened the door to a new civilizational frequency.

In Chapter 2, we diagnosed why the inherited leadership OS is failing, attempting to run exponential realities on linear code.

In Chapter 3, we stepped beyond servant leadership, introducing resonance as the ground of next-level leadership.

In Chapter 4, we entered the new Renaissance and showed how growth at the edge supports creation.

In Chapter 5, we retired the myth of the solo hero and redefined leadership as collective emergence, rooted in trust and coherence.

Now we reach the heart of the matter: making decisions.

At its core, leadership means making choices.

Decisions drive leadership and animate every system.

Each choice you make affects your culture and future possibilities.

Every pause and change adds something new to the future you are building.

Every clear or unclear moment reshapes your story.

Desert Navigation at Night

As a young army lieutenant and infantry platoon leader, I trained in the California Mojave Desert's National Training Center, a simulated war zone designed to test decision-making under pressure. Our assignment was to act as the adversary, or opposition force, and push army leadership to their limits when certainty disappears.

Night operations defined our training. As we looked through night-vision goggles, the desert took on a green glow. My soldiers advanced with assurance, relying on our maps and drills.

One night, I led the platoon across open ground, senses wide, cloaked in a very dark night. Then a sharp rattle shattered the stillness.

At first, I registered only a rustle in a thick sagebush. Then the pattern resolved: a six-foot rattlesnake emerged, fat, coiled, and ready to strike, its tail a living boundary between safety and consequence.

I acted instinctively, signaling the platoon to stop, right hand in the air with a clenched fist at the end of a L-shaped elbow. We faced a choice: Move forward and risk a bite. Stop, lose time, and risk potential detection. Or adapt. Our plan and risks had changed with the sound of a rattle.

While this incident was minor in the broader mission, it was a real decision point with effects beyond that moment.

That night etched a deeper lesson: Leadership is not forged in the clarity of daylight, but in the ambiguity of darkness, where information is partial, terrain is shifting, and hazards emerge from what we take for granted. Here, the rattlesnake serves as a metaphor for the unforeseen risks that can disrupt our assumptions and plans. Every founder and company builder has felt it.

Leading in the human+machine era is a similar navigation. Our AI insights, data metrics, and agentic feedback act like night-vision goggles. They reveal certain patterns and data, but never provide a complete view of the complex landscape. The ground itself is shifting with surprises, like rattlesnakes hidden in the parts we cannot yet see.

In these conditions, *coherence* is essential for adapting and staying relevant.

Decision Bottlenecks in a Nonlinear World

As we saw in Chapter 2, the human operating system strains under exponential pressure. Nowhere is that strain more visible than in the crucible of decision-making.

For much of the last century, leaders followed a linear playbook: Gather data, analyze, apply expertise/experience, and issue orders. It worked in an industrial era, when markets moved at the pace of people and annual planning cycles offered stability. Today, waiting for certainty is itself the greatest risk.

Executives know this intuitively. Bain & Company reports that senior leaders spend nearly 40% of their time making decisions. Yet 61% say slow processes cost them growth opportunities.[67] McKinsey found that organizations that make decisions quickly are twice as likely to outperform financially. Yet fewer than one in five leaders claim their company excels in this area.[68] PwC calls these decision bottlenecks—places where analysis multiplies but choices stall.[69]

The old way worked for control and order, but now we must handle change—exponential and often multidirectional change. Waiting for perfect data means the goal may change before we act.

Jeff Bezos reframed the act itself. He distinguishes between Type 1 decisions (irreversible, high stakes) and Type 2 decisions (reversible, frequent). Type 2 calls should be made fast and often, he argues, because *most decisions are two-way doors*.[70] Netflix co-founder Reed Hastings pushes his teams to move at 70% confidence because aiming for 90% means the opportunity has passed.

This new world asks leaders to act quickly. Notice changes and respond clearly when it matters. The goal is to be ready for change, not to know everything.

Decisions as Systemic Learning

The old way saw decisions as final. The new way sees them as ongoing feedback, where each choice helps the system grow.

Peter Senge, systems scientist and senior lecturer at the MIT Sloan School of Management, described the *learning organization* as a system that views every choice as feedback into the whole.[71] Every decision becomes an experiment that generates information, which, if sensed and integrated, accelerates adaptation.

The data echoes this shift. Bain found that organizations embracing rapid, iterative decision cycles outpaced peers in both execution and trust; it was the discipline of closing loops and learning in real time.

Netflix illustrates the principle. Reed Hastings's 2011 decision to split the DVD and streaming businesses was a disaster at first, costing the company eight hundred thousand subscribers in one quarter. But because the decision was treated as an experimental *loop* rather than a *verdict*, Netflix adjusted quickly. Within three years, it led the world in streaming and original content.[72]

Amazon systematized this with the Type 1/Type 2 framework. Type 2 decisions are pushed to the edge, made fast, and corrected if wrong. Type 1 decisions require alignment and caution. This segmentation prevents overload while maintaining velocity.

Leaders who approach decisions as learning loops rather than fixed verdicts build organizations capable of rapid evolution in the face of complexity.

Practice Box: Map Your Decision Signals

1. Recall three major decisions from the past quarter.
2. Note your first physical cue—jaw tension, shallow breath, tight chest.
3. Map the outcome: Did the decision close a loop and create learning, or did the loop remain open and drain energy?
4. Identify one ritual you can add (pause, breath, team check-in) to improve loop closure.

Leadership Neuroscience: The Biology of Decisions

Decision-making is not merely cognitive; it is embodied.

Leaders transmit through their nervous systems, broadcasting a signal that shapes the collective field. The state you inhabit becomes the atmosphere your team breathes.

Amy Arnsten at Yale showed that stress rapidly degrades prefrontal capacity, leaving the amygdala to drive reflexive behavior.[73] Shields, Sazma, and Yonelinas confirmed that acute stress shrinks working memory and cognitive flexibility, which are the functions that business strategy depends on.[74]

Stephen Porges' *Polyvagal Theory* explains why: The vagus nerve is constantly asking three questions: "Am I safe? Am I connected? Can I act?" If the body answers, "No," the system defaults to survival, narrowing perspective.[75]

This biology is contagious. Research in interpersonal neurobiology reveals that teams synchronize their physiology within minutes.[76] Shopify's Red Friday recovery, outlined in Chapter 2, proved it in practice: Organizational speed follows physiological coherence.

Leaders who manage their own bodies help teams feel calm. Leaders who ignore this create confusion.

The Decision Compass

So, how do leaders move from uncertainty to clarity without paralysis or panic?

The Decision Compass is not a checklist; it's a tool for moving from chaos to order, over and over.

1. **Sense the Field**

   Start by paying attention to subtle cues. Early threats can change your direction significantly.

2. **Gather Signals**

   Use both data and what people at the edges know. Groups that listen to many voices do better. Hearing from many sources is vital in complex situations.

3. **Embody Stillness**

   Pause. Align your head, heart, and gut. That is, bring your **thoughts (head), values and emotions (heart), and instincts or intuition (gut)** into coherence before taking action. Harvard researchers found that leaders who practiced two minutes of slow breathing before critical meetings showed measurable increases in cognitive flexibility.[77]

At Army Ranger School, we called this a listening stop, a brief tactical halt in movement where the patrol stops to observe and listen for signs of the enemy or other relevant activity before continuing forward.

Distill direction from the noise. The aim is not certainty but coherence—

alignment across body, mind, and context. Most decisions are made in the fog. The real work is to find resonance, meaning a sense of underlying rightness and alignment, not to pursue perfection. Steve Jobs and Elon Musk are masters, separating signal from noise in real time (the absolute present moment) and all the time.

4. **Commit Fully**

Half-decisions leak energy. They create open loops in attention, pulling cognitive and emotional resources into limbo. Unresolved choices foster ambiguity, stall execution, and quietly drain momentum. In low-trust environments, teams hesitate to commit, waiting for clarity or cover, and in that waiting, inertia sets in.

5. **Communicate Cleanly**

Signal decisions clearly. *Harvard Business Review* reports that transparent decision communication boosts execution speed by 55%.[78]

Practice Box: Map Your Team's Triggers

1. Recall three recent breakdowns.
2. Identify the first collective signal—Slack chatter, silence, over-analysis.
3. Name the trigger: deadline, shock, conflict.
4. Build a reset ritual for that pattern.

Organizational Design Cues

Even the most agile leaders and teams will stall if the organization's architecture is designed for overload. Structure is not neutral; it shapes behavior and possibility.

- **Distributed authority:** Amazon's two-pizza teams reduce bottlenecks.[79] Wharton found that distributed firms are 34% faster on innovation speed.[80]
- **Transparent information flow:** Atlassian's Playbook and Shopify's radical data layers enable edge action without top-down delay.

- **Cadence over calendar:** Replace rigid quarters with adaptive cycles. Bain reports firms using shorter cycles are 30% faster at integrating new data.[81]
- **State-first leadership training:** Treat nervous-system literacy as a core competency. Elite military units train state agility with biofeedback. Forward-thinking companies are adding coherence practices to executive development.

These interventions reinforce each other, especially when combined with individual practices described in Chapter 2: breathwork steadying the individual, coherence huddles stabilizing the team, and distributed sensing keeping the system adaptive. They create a metaloop of resilience. Physiology scaffolds psychology, and strategy finds its ground.

Closing the Loop

AI evolves through supervised and unsupervised feedback loops, and so do leaders and their teams. Every decision is a signal sent into the system. When the loop closes—then is sensed, integrated, and adjusted—learning compounds. When it stays open, entropy takes the lead.

This is the leader's truth: Decisions are not finish lines but pulses in a living system. The rattlesnake in the brush is more than a threat; it is a signal, a teacher at the edge of the known.

The nervous system that governs each decision becomes the same instrument that governs every act of creation.

Breath becomes bandwidth. The pause becomes performance. Structure becomes a signal. Each is a lever for coherence amid complexity.

Practice Box: Daily Decision Reset

At day's end, ask:
- "What decisions did I make?"
- "What state was I in?"
- "Did I close loops or leave them open?"
- "What one reset will strengthen tomorrow's signal?"

Ten minutes a day builds the muscle memory of coherence.

Bridge to Chapter 7—The Next Signal

The anatomy of a decision reveals the inner architecture of leadership in complexity. We've seen how decisions collapse when physiology falters, how organizations lose coherence, and how breath, pause, and structure can restore the system's momentum. Yet this anatomy is only half the story. Leaders are not just decision-makers; they are the tuning instruments themselves, translating inner state into outer design.

Leaders who master the anatomy of decision are not merely faster. They become architects of coherence in an age of noise, pattern decoders preparing to navigate the inner operating system of leadership itself.

CHAPTER 7

Better at You, Better at What You Do

"Get better at being you, and everything you do gets better. That's not philosophy. That's physics."—BEN POTVIN, *former Cirque du Soleil Performer/Coach, Chief Creative Officer, Liminal Collective*

I n the last chapter, we became pattern decoders, tracing the anatomy of a decision, spotting where coherence frays, and noticing how elemental practices like breath, pause, and structure can quickly reset the system. We saw how flow, once lost, returns through simple, embodied resets.

Now the journey pivots from decoding patterns to applying insight. Up to this point, we've mapped the leader's dance with complexity, which has revealed legacy code, naming the myths and stepping into presence. Here, we cross a threshold, moving from awareness into embodied application, where insight becomes action.

This chapter reveals the inner mechanics of leadership. Level 7 leadership is rooted not in tactics or structures but in the leader's self-mastery and adaptability in our rapidly evolving world. It is your ability to regulate your own state, align your actions, and adapt that forms the true starting point for transformational impact.

Where the Industrial Revolution pushed bodies to their limit, the Intelligence Age requires an upgrade of a different kind: not hustling harder, but cultivating deeper presence. The focus shifts from overworking the human system to attuning it for clarity, creativity, and imagination.

Harder, Faster, and More

During the Industrial Revolution, when technology outpaced humans, the reflex was simple: **Work harder.**

In the late nineteenth and early twentieth centuries, factory workers endured twelve- to sixteen-hour days. Children as young as ten spun cotton. To keep up, society reached for chemical shortcuts, like cocaine-filled tonics, opiates, and the original Coca-Cola, laced with coca-leaf extract. Harvard historian David Courtwright chronicles this era in *Forces of Habit*.

Efficiency was worshipped. Exhaustion was sanctified.

That logic still echoes in the 9-6-6 work schedule, the popularity of energy drinks like Monster and Red Bull, and hustle culture that praises developers who work for thirty-six-hour pushes. From Coca-Cola to Red Bull, the message persists: "Outrun the velocity of reality."

Today, we find the old equation collapsing. Robotics and AI no longer just outpace our bodies, they now surpass specialized cognition. Assembly lines hum with robotic welders, while algorithms analyze contracts, generate code, and summarize meetings. What the factory once did to the arm, AI is now doing to the mind.

Analysis from sources like McKinsey estimates that up to 375 million people may need to switch occupations by 2030.[82] Goldman Sachs Research projects that generative AI could ultimately automate about one-quarter of work tasks in advanced economies.[83]

Amid these shifts, a critical question emerges: When machines can calculate and predict, what remains rare? **Human imagination. Human adaptability. Human presence.**

These are the emerging frontiers. The emphasis for humans is shifting, from speed and specialization to the capacity to slow down, reflect inward, and create from a place of coherence. Take large language models (LLMs), for example. While machines handle scale and repetition, humans are essential for *inbound sensing* (What matters?) and *outbound guidance* (What should be done?). Machines offer directionless velocity. Humans offer coherence.

The current edge comes from those who can sense and influence the environment within themselves and the systems they support.

Leadership Is an Inside Job

Leadership is not born in the boardroom. It begins in the nervous system, in the subtle signals that shape how we show up and what we transmit to those around us.

Neuroscientists from leading centers have shown what monks and martial artists long intuited: Your state is your company's thermostat.

When you are reactive, your team contracts. When you are centered, they expand. Brittle leadership is mirrored as tension, while presence fosters creativity and resilience.

Presence is not a soft skill. It is the strategic infrastructure, the invisible architecture that underpins everything else.

When your inner state is aligned, your leadership amplifies. Coherence is contagious. When you achieve it, everything you touch begins to vibrate at that same frequency.

You cannot build trust across teams if you haven't built trust with yourself.

You cannot scale adaptability if you cannot embody it daily.

You cannot sustain velocity if your nervous system is locked in survival mode.

The primary obstacle to adaptability is not external; it is neither technology nor talent. It is the leader's personal capacity to guide themselves through change, setting the resonance that shapes the collective.

The Triangle of Transcendence

Every leader stands inside a psychological triangle.

One corner holds insecurity and imposter syndrome.

Another holds confidence, sometimes inflated.

Above both, humility hovers. Confidence without humility becomes ego. Insecurity without reflection becomes paralysis.

Humility transforms both, anchoring strength and dissolving fear. It is the field from which authentic leadership arises.

Level 7 leaders live here. They don't need to be heroes, nor do they collapse under doubt. They're in a space where grounded humility opens the field so collective brilliance can emerge.

The Collapse of the Lone Genius

As we reflected on in Chapter 5, our culture idolizes the lone genius: Leonardo da Vinci sketching by candlelight, Einstein scribbling equations in isolation, Jobs unveiling the iPhone.

But genius is very seldom solitary.

Jobs had Ive. Einstein had his circle of peers. Every breakthrough is collective.

At Apple's design studio under Jony Ive, engineers and designers improvised in real time. The iPhone and iPad weren't born from a single mind but from the resonance of many.

Years later, at a meditation retreat, I sat beside Ive's successor, Evans Hankey, not as an executive but as a human doing inner work. The future of design, like the future of leadership, is being shaped not just in labs but also in silence.

Level 7 leaders know their role is not to be the genius, but to architect the conditions where genius becomes inevitable. Their work is to shape the field so that brilliance is drawn in and amplified.

The Chemistry of Flow and Collective Brilliance

When presence stabilizes, something extraordinary happens: The chemistry of collaboration changes. As time bends, meetings energize instead of draining, and ideas spark instead of fizzling.

Empirical studies of high-performing groups show that conversational energy, engagement, and exploration predict team performance, an insight popularized by MIT's Human Dynamics Lab.

This isn't mysticism; it's measurable physiology.

Dopamine fuels motivation. Oxytocin deepens trust. Serotonin steadies mood. Endorphins sustain resilience.

Teams in sustained flow are rewiring themselves for future brilliance. Each shared success lays down a new neural pathway for what becomes possible next.

The Leader as Guardian of the Field

Level 7 leaders are not the stars of the show. They are the **guardians of the field.**

Their role is to **tune the invisible architecture** of the system:

- **Rituals,** like how meetings begin or off-sites are run
- **Rhythms,** such as weekly cadences or planning cycles
- **Spaces,** whether physical (a meeting room) or digital (Zoom norms and presence)

All of these shape the conditions in which coherence can emerge.

Research from MIT's Human Dynamics Lab shows that high-performing teams share **richer, more balanced interaction patterns**—and these signals can be shaped by a leader's presence and design choices.

At West Point, we learned early that **tone at the top is everything**. How the commander shows up is how the troops show up. The leader's nervous system sets the baseline:

Transmit fear, and the team mirrors fear.

Embody calm clarity, and the system harmonizes around that signal.

The leader's state *is* the culture.

To be clear, this isn't about stripping away authenticity or vulnerability. In fact, leaders who embody these traits **amplify trust** and cultivate stability through transparency.

Coherence is not about perfection. It's about honesty that resonates.

From Hustle Rooms to Flow Rooms

Hustle rooms deplete.

Flow rooms are environments that generate energy and creativity.

Consider creative crucibles like Pixar's Braintrust, where feedback is direct yet safe, built on open trust and a focus on resonance rather than ego, or the "pause, reset, reframe" rituals that cutting-edge companies use in high-pressure sprints. The difference lies in more than strategy alone.

It all comes down to the **state**.

When leaders model coherence, they create an atmosphere where critique becomes curiosity and tension becomes creative energy. The energy once spent managing anxiety is now liberated as fuel for innovation.

Whole-Body Intelligence and Sensing

The new frontier of leadership is not about thinking faster, but about sensing and feeling with greater intelligence.

The next generation of leaders will not simply analyze complexity—they will attune to it. They will learn to read the signals of their own nervous system and sense the coherence of their teams the way a conductor hears harmony in an orchestra.

Multiple research streams converge here.

The HeartMath Institute's monographs describe the heart's intrinsic nervous system and its role in *physiological coherence* as ordered, sine-wave-like heart-rhythm patterns associated with synchronization across respiratory, blood-pressure, and brain-wave systems.

At the core is heart-rate variability (HRV). Neuroscientists, such as Julian Thayer, have shown through meta-analyses of neuroimaging studies that HRV tracks prefrontal regulatory networks and executive function.[84] HRV predicts adaptability and emotional balance under stress.

There's also a resonance phenomenon. The cardiorespiratory system has a natural frequency around 0.1 Hz. When we breathe slowly and evenly (about five seconds in, five seconds out) while cultivating an elevated emotion, such as gratitude, HRV often shifts into a coherent 0.1 Hz rhythm. Studies link this state to improved cognitive performance and emotional stability, and, over time, to a higher baseline of calm clarity.

Related work in **interoception**—the brain's ability to sense and interpret internal bodily signals, such as breath, heartbeat, and visceral state—explains why this matters for leaders. *It's what allows a leader to recognize a spike in heart rate before a big decision or to notice tension in the gut during a difficult conversation—signals that often carry insight before thought can.*

As coherence rises, teams synchronize more easily. This is a social-coherence effect documented in group HRV studies.

The HeartMath Institute calls this heart intelligence. It is the flow of intuitive awareness that arises when heart, mind, and emotion align. In practice, it's not supernatural. It's mechanical and trainable.

Vignette: Feeling the Field

After reading *Breaking the Habit of Being Yourself* by Joe Dispenza, studying the HeartMath Institute's work, and exploring Itzhak Bentov's *Stalking the Wild Pendulum*, I began to see the invisible fabric connecting physics, biology, and leadership.

There was science behind what I had always felt but couldn't name, a living current of coherence moving through people, teams, and systems.

During my year studying with Joseph Jaworski, co-author of *Presence* and author of *Source*, I heard Joseph speak of this field of energy many times.

At Janus Henderson, Pacific Current Group, TIFIN, Vantage Discovery, and Grid Aero, I saw how the collective mood of a room would shift when a single person entered. The energy is either scattered or harmonized. You can feel it.

Looking back, I realize what I was sensing wasn't mystical; it was scientifically measurable. The same field that synchronizes flocks of birds and firing neurons also links human systems.

As president of my class at West Point, a platoon leader, and later a CEO and board member, I was feeling the resonance that coherence science now validates.

What I once called gut instinct or leadership presence was actually a coherent field. It can be felt, measured, trained, and taught. Once I understood that, everything changed.

Leadership wasn't about control; it became about energetic stewardship.

The most powerful leaders don't dominate the field; they stabilize it. They become tuning forks for coherence itself.

Since then, I've practiced and coached coherence daily. The results have been deeper trust, faster alignment, clearer decisions, and a felt sense of collective flow that no management theory alone can produce.

When coherence becomes embodied, leadership ceases to be about control. It becomes about **resonance**, creating the conditions for intelligence to arise *through us*, not *from us*.

Practices for Cultivating Whole-Body Intelligence

HEART-FOCUSED BREATHING

Bring attention to the heart area. Inhale and exhale slowly (about five seconds each) while evoking gratitude or compassion. Continue for several minutes to synchronize rhythm and emotion. (See HeartMath's *Science of the Heart* for full technique.[85])

MICRO PAUSES

Before key interactions, take twenty seconds to sense internal rhythm: breath, chest, gut. Notice whether you're coherent or fragmented before speaking.

RESONANCE JOURNALING

Track moments of clarity versus reactivity; note the sensations that preceded each. Patterns soon emerge.

TEAM COHERENCE RITUALS

Open meetings with thirty seconds of collective breathing and a shared intention. Ask, "What does our group body feel right now?" and adjust from that awareness. (See MIT Human Dynamics Lab for data on team interaction patterns.)

FEEDBACK LOOPS

Use HRV biofeedback (e.g., Inner Balance, emWave) to track coherence over time. HRV-neuroimaging meta-analyses explain why this correlates with better top-down regulation.

Integrating Coherence in Leadership Flow

Whole-body intelligence is not a luxury reserved for the esoteric. It is the foundation for resilient and creative leadership.

Leaders who practice coherence notice shifts before they become crises. They sense the undercurrents not through OKR and FinOps reports, but through embodied awareness. Their calm becomes a stabilizing frequency, allowing others to think clearly and act boldly.

The heart plays a central role in this process, functioning as both a receiver and transmitter of energetic and emotional information. Research from the HeartMath Institute shows that the heart generates an electromagnetic field over fifty times stronger than the brain's, measurable up to three feet away.[86] This field not only senses others' emotional states but also influences them. A coherent heart rhythm broadcasts a signal of safety and stability, helping others regulate and align—often without a word being spoken.

Over time, coherence becomes second nature, a new baseline of being.

Decisions begin to flow from resonance rather than reaction. Presence itself becomes a living strategy.

When a leader holds coherence, the room shifts, not by command, but through the field they generate.

From Inner to Outer Coherence

The last Industrial Revolution tried to solve overload with cocaine and caffeine.

This one calls for coherence. It is the new operating system for the Intelligence Age.

This is the blueprint for leading at the edge of the known, where the map ends and new possibilities begin.

When leaders master presence, they regulate the field. When they cultivate humility, they unlock collective brilliance.

The advantage is not speed but harmony.

The fuel is not cortisol but presence.

Presence fuels coherence.

Coherence scales into consciousness.

In the next chapter, we'll explore how leaders translate inner mastery into organizational coherence, and how entire companies can learn, adapt, and evolve at today's pace of change.

CHAPTER 8

Beacons,
Not Blueprints

"The map is not the territory."—ALFRED KORZYBSKI

S enior leaders grounded in core values create clarity that cascades across the organization. At the highest level, effective leadership is less about micromanagement and more about cultivating an adaptive environment, one that continuously senses, decides, and acts in alignment with emerging priorities.

In today's human+machine era, organizational scale depends on signal strength and adaptability, not size. High-performing companies rapidly sense and respond to subtle shifts, integrating strategic human judgment with AI to maintain competitive velocity. Strategy has evolved from static planning to a continually updating process, shaped by both executive insight and advanced technologies.

The Legacy Playbook: Jim Collins and Strategy That Sticks

To understand this shift, we begin with what shaped so many of today's leaders: Jim Collins's *Good to Great*. Two ideas from that book became foundational to strategy:

- **BHAG (Big Hairy Audacious Goal):** A bold, long-term objective that rallies the organization. Think: Land a man on the moon. A BHAG is directional, magnetic, and energizing.
- **The Hedgehog Concept:** Strategy at the intersection of three circles:
  - » What you're deeply passionate about
  - » What can you be best at in the world?
  - » What drives your economic engine

Collins taught leaders to discover their hedgehog, set a BHAG, and turn the flywheel, a consistent, disciplined effort that compounds over time.[87]

This model thrived in an era of slow change, when markets were steady, skills endured, and assumptions held their shape. But the landscape has shifted beneath our feet.

The Strategy Half-Life

Today, strategy decays faster than alignment can catch up. Its half-life is measured in months, not years. Technology evolves in weeks. AI accelerates adoption across industries. Consider:

- ChatGPT hit one hundred million users in two months.
- Claude now processes over 25 billion API calls every month, with about 45 % of that traffic coming from enterprise customers."[88]
- The World Economic Forum predicts 44% of workforce skills will be disrupted in five years.[89]

In organizations, even the most carefully crafted plans can feel outdated before the next off-site. Strategy loses relevance not from error, but because the terrain it mapped has already transformed.

The challenge is not with the frameworks but with the cadence at which senior teams apply them. Annual strategic planning is insufficient in a world where market dynamics shift weekly. Executives must ensure that operating rhythms become as adaptive and responsive as today's realities demand.

Where *Good to Great* Still Wins, and Where It Doesn't

The genius of Collins still applies:

- Purpose matters.
- Focus compounds.
- Vision galvanizes.

But the rules of motion have changed:

- **Cadence:** Annual strategy cycles can't keep pace with monthly disruptions.
- **Granularity:** Value emerges at the product or pod level, not just enterprise scale.
- **Feedback physics:** Signals now travel faster than traditional governance can absorb.

The frameworks remain powerful but only when paired with the adaptive rhythms required by today's reality. Strategy must act as a dynamic, responsive signal attuned to the present.

BHAG 2.0: Beacons, Not Blueprints

A BHAG served as a North Star for decades. Now its direction stays essential, but the path must flex and adapt in real time, updating as needed.

Design principles for beaconed strategy:

- Be precise about the *why*, flexible about the *how*.
- Time-box assumptions: Tie them to thresholds in behavior, costs, or talent.
- Set kill switches: Decide in advance what triggers a pivot.
- Refresh intent quickly, within twenty-four hours of a major signal shift.

Remember, a beacon is not a blueprint. It acts as a compass, steady, visible, and magnetic, pulling us forward as our path adapts. The key takeaway: Set a clear direction, but let your approach shift as reality evolves.

Hedgehog 2.0: The Three Circles in Motion

The Hedgehog Concept framework still holds. But now, each circle moves:

- **Passion** shows up as energy density, deep-work hours, builder NPS, and team vitality.
- **Best-in-world** shifts as AI levels the playing field. The differentiator is your *learning rate*.
- **The economic engine** gains new levers: model efficiency, usage-based pricing, and AI-driven margins.

In essence, the hedgehog panel keeps you honest about how your passion, learning, and economic engine are moving. Key takeaway: Use it as an ongoing dashboard, not just an annual exercise.

The Power of Tipping Points and Thin Slices

Big change starts small. A model outperforms quietly. A pod ships two times faster. A product catches unexpected traction.

These thin slices, when noticed early, become hidden advantages. Presence closes the gap between sensing and acting. The organizations that thrive move at the velocity of their smallest signals.

From Habits to Systems: The Atomic Advantage

James Clear's *Atomic Habits* reframes change as identity-driven:

Identity → Process → Outcome

At enterprise scale, the same logic applies:

- **Identity-based habits:** Name who you're becoming ("We are a learning company") and build rituals to match—daily stand-ups with intention-setting, weekly reflection rounds, postmortems centered on learning, or opening meetings with a coherence breath.
- **Environmental design:** Make right action easy, embed AI, surface data.
- **Habit stacking:** Tie new behaviors to existing cadences.
- **Immediate feedback:** Celebrate micro wins. Reward iteration as well as results.

This is how desired behavior becomes default and coherence is woven into the system's fabric. Takeaway: At scale, system design, not heroic willpower, sustains positive change.

CRIT: Prompt as Strategy

In *The AI-Driven Leader*, Geoff Woods offers CRIT:[90]

- **Context:** What's happening?
- **Role:** What expertise should AI take?
- **Interview:** Let the model ask questions to deepen understanding.
- **Task:** Request grounded output.

When used well, AI becomes a co-designer—surfacing edge signals, reframing assumptions, and rehearsing possible futures before they unfold. Paraphrasing an approach advocated by Geoff Woods, here's how to frame our market and margin pressures: act as a strategic investor. Ask probing questions about risk and timing, and provide pros and cons for each product bet.[91] AI as a decision-maker has shown mixed results; AI as a coherent thought partner with human agency is much more powerful.

Woods calls it "designing with AI, not delegating to AI."[92] It marks the shift from command-and-control to real-time co-creation.

Strategy in the Attention Economy

Strategy now lives in the current of culture. Attention outpaces decisions. Platforms shape perception. A product may remain the same, yet its narrative can shift in a single night.

Social signals become telemetry. Digital behavior becomes pattern data. When paired with AI acceleration, test-and-learn cycles can run weekly if your systems are tuned to support it.

If they don't, teams may sense the truth but remain blocked by old approvals or rigid processes.

Strategy sets the signal. Cadence creates the motion. In a world shaped by cultural currents and technological acceleration, synchronizing strategy and execution becomes paramount.

Picture a Tuesday huddle. Over the weekend, a competitor shifted the category. Finance is steady. Product is alarmed. Marketing needs a new story by Friday.

The old playbook would wait. The new one moves.

The question is no longer "What's the plan?" It's "What rhythm keeps us in sync with emergent reality?"

The Two-Speed Company

- **Speed 1:** Beaconed direction, the steady "Why?"
- **Speed 2:** Live cycle, the responsive "What's next?"

This approach allows coherence to scale while enabling adaptation at the edge. Key takeaway: Scaling comes from balancing clear direction and agile adaptation.

Pods That Ship

Owner-led pods collapse the distance between sensing and acting. No handoffs, no delay. Just movement. A pod is a small, cross-functional, owner-led team with end-to-end responsibility for sensing, deciding, building, and delivering a specific outcome. It contains within it the authority, skills, and accountability required to move from insight to execution without escalation or handoff.

McKinsey's organizational research shows that speed comes from fewer handoffs, smaller teams, and higher decision authority at the edge. In practice, leaders often experience this as multi-fold acceleration when compared with traditional hierarchies. At TIFIN, I consistently promoted smaller objectives, smaller teams, and shorter timelines, which allowed us to learn faster—oftentimes less comfortably, but much faster. Pods would learn in weeks what it would take a quarter to learn in a less agile structure.

Six-Week Cycles: Shape, Build, Show

A cadence that turns signal into action:
- **Week 0 – Shape:** Frame the problem, appetite, and risk.
- **Weeks 1–5 – Build:** Eliminate noise. One pod, one bet.
- **Week 6 – Show:** Demo to customers. Decide: kill, scale, or evolve.

Every six weeks: a decision pulse, strategy as living motion. Principal takeaway: Rapid, regular cycles keep strategy relevant and teams engaged.

Governance for Speed: Intent over Approvals

General Stanley McChrystal called it "shared consciousness + empowered execution."[93]

Instead of chasing consensus, flood the org with context. Then trust local nodes to move.

Lightweight rituals:

- **Daily intel (15 mins.):** Share what changed, what matters, what you'll try.
- **Weekly decision market (30–45 mins.):** Pods surface key decisions. Leaders offer context, not control.
- **Monthly portfolio review:** Decide based on evidence, not inertia.

This is how adaptive strategy breathes, exhaling what is complete and inhaling what is next.

Templates That Anchor Motion

These aren't ceremonial documents. They're living tools:

- **Beacon sheet:** Why we exist · Key assumptions · Kill switches · Refresh cadence
- **Hedgehog panel:** Passion · Learning velocity · Economic trend
- **Six-week bet card:** Problem · Appetite · Risks · Owner · Definition of "done"
- **OKR overlay:** Objective as beacon · Key results as signal

These tools translate strategy into breathwork. They help release what's complete and draw in what's emerging. Main takeaway: Use templates to anchor learning and momentum, not just documentation.

Your First Sixty Days

This is not transformation theater. It is a rhythm reset—helping the organization learn to breathe as a single field.

- **Days 0–7:** Publish beacon and first hedgehog panel. Launch two pods. Baseline learning velocity.
- **Days 8–21:** Shape your first bet. Launch daily intel and decision market. Set pod norms.
- **Days 22–42:** Remove two friction points. Show in-progress work. Track learning speed.
- **Days 43–60:** Ship. Learn. Decide. Refresh beacon and hedgehog assumptions.

These moves set the tone and show that rhythm is the new operating system. The clear takeaway: Focus on building adaptive rhythms for lasting transformation.

Why This Works: The Human Reason

People do not need perfect certainty. They need meaningful direction and agency in the week they are living.

The two-speed model gives both the long pull of purpose and the short-cycle momentum that makes work feel alive.

By embracing this shift, executive leaders amplify organizational intelligence. Human and machine rhythms become aligned, enabling leadership to set the frequency for coherence, focus, and responsiveness.

The company becomes a signal.

The system moves.

Leadership as Frequency

We have moved from the anatomy of a decision to the architecture of motion—from coherence in the individual to coherence in the system.

But coherence can scale further.

When the leader becomes a frequency—a steady tone harmonizing human and machine intelligence—the organization shifts from a collection of teams to a single, living field.

That's where we go next. Chapter 9 explores the leader as a signal source: the human frequency that synchronizes creativity, trust, and intelligence at enterprise scale.

CHAPTER 9

Leadership As Resonance

"Motion without memory is noise. Feedback makes rhythm possible."
— Level 7 Leadership

C hapter 8 covered the visible architecture: the beaconed BHAG, the living hedgehog panel, pods with end-to-end ownership, and the six-week pulse. This pulse turns vision into motion.

The structure is only the scaffolding. What animates a living organization is its capacity to learn. Each feedback cycle fine-tunes the next, gradually transforming ongoing movement into a form of organizational intelligence. This is like music, where repeated practice turns motion into rhythm and awareness.

We're stepping across a new threshold: moving from simple motion to motion that remembers, where every action leaves a trace that the system can sense and build upon.

Without feedback, activity becomes noise. Busy actions lose meaning, and important learning is forgotten. The system can no longer recall what once worked.

With feedback, each action is like a note in a musical composition, with every note echoing forward to influence the next. The organization starts to work in harmony, adjusting itself as it goes, like an orchestra tuning while it plays.

When feedback systems are alive, organizational learning accelerates even faster than market shifts. The organization develops a sense like musical intonation. It has an instinct to adjust quickly, staying in harmony as circumstances change. This is how the abstract becomes practical: making resonance, like musical harmony, tangible and measurable.

What Feedback Means in a Two-Speed Company

Feedback is not a suggestion box or a quarterly survey. It connects a living, sensing organization. Feedback is how tone travels from the edge to the center and back, alive and clear.

In practice, it means three things:

1. **Instrumented work:** Instrumented work refers to systematically tracking actions, decisions, and experiments so that each one can be evaluated. This includes leaving a trace—a hypothesis, a time stamp, and an expectation of learning.
2. **Fast routing:** Fast routing means ensuring that important signals flow directly to where action occurs—such as moving from pod to portfolio to platform—without unnecessary gatekeeping or filtration.
3. **Time-boxed interpretation:** Time-boxed interpretation is the practice of evaluating information and making sense of it within set time frames, ensuring meaning is made rhythmically—through daily intel, weekly decision markets, and six-week shows—instead of reactively.

When these elements are present, feedback shifts from concept to felt rhythm, a pulse inside the week. People sense when the system is in tune: Decisions land with clarity, meetings contract, trust expands.

The Feedback Backbone: Six Questions, Always in Order

Feedback isn't a ritual; it's a rhythm. The healthiest organizations treat learning as a living pulse, powered by structured curiosity rather than endless opinion.

The following six questions form that pulse: a disciplined conversation that turns noise into insight, insight into action, and action into progress. Run them in sequence, consistently, and you'll transform feedback from a reactive chore into the backbone of adaptive intelligence in your learning organization.

1. **What changed?** Name the signal. Is it customer behavior, reliability, cost, competitor move?
2. **What does it likely mean?** Offer a one-sentence interpretation, provisional but clear.
3. **What will you try?** Pick the smallest experiment that could generate the next piece of truth.
4. **What must be true?** Make assumptions explicit; state the guardrail.
5. **Who owns the first two steps?** Name them; assign time.
6. **When do you revisit?** Set the next inspection date. Close the loop before you open it.

Run these six questions weekly, and you're in the feedback business. Each loop becomes a single heartbeat in the organization's learning body.

Routing Signal to the Edge: Keeping Translation Cost Low

Most organizations have a lot of data, but clarity remains rare. The real shortage is shared understanding, not information.

Signals move up hierarchies through slides and summaries. With each handoff, they lose their original tone. By the time they come back, they are abstractions, and resonance is lost in translation.

Three design moves keep the sound clean:

1. **Make "raw" visible:** Let pods see unedited user interactions: recordings, logs, notes. If a summarized chart changed a decision last cycle, show the raw source this cycle. Focus on real sound over remixed echoes.
2. **Default to push:** Keep a short signal digest. What changed? What's the likely meaning? What are the anomalies? Send it into the channels where teams already live. Feedback should arrive like a welcome rhythm, not homework.
3. **Name the owner:** Each key result (KR) or flow metric

has one steward accountable for freshness and interpretation. Ambiguity is the silence between notes. Ownership keeps the music alive. When teams engage directly with unfiltered signals, they respond in harmony rather than discord. Experiments sharpen, and performance theater recedes.

Shortening the Customer-Signal Half-Life

The best measure of organizational resonance is how quickly real customer feedback reaches those who can act on it. If it takes weeks, you're running a theater.

If it takes hours to learn, learning compounds that time.

Consider the following ways to shorten the half-life:

- **Mid-cycle shows:** Do not wait for Week 6. At Week 3, show a rough demo to real users. Capture what surprised you, what changed your confidence, and what you will try next.
- **Feedback lanes:** Create a fast lane for safe-to-try tweaks—copy, micro flows, feature flags. Let pods ship daily micro experiments; reserve ceremonies for irreversible moves.
- **Close the loop publicly:** When a customer request drives a change, tell them. Visibility teaches everyone what responsiveness feels like.
- **Favor early exposure over polish:** The aim is not applause, but speed *to truth.* The sooner reality enters the room, the sooner the organization can retune itself.

The speed at which truth travels defines competitive advantage. When customer signals move freely, without distortion or delay, teams stop guessing and start compounding insight. The organizations that thrive are not those with the most data, but those with the shortest distance between hearing and acting. Shorten that half-life, and you turn feedback from a lagging indicator into a living current of progress.

Instrument Ideas, Not Just Deployments

Traditional scoreboards measure output, like features shipped and revenue booked.

Learning systems score the composition process itself—how ideas move from spark to signal.

One entrepreneur I advised called this running plays, like an American football team. He asked, "Which plays worked and which did not, and why?

Here are a few practical tools that help teams instrument their idea flow and make learning visible throughout the process:

- **Hypothesis ledger:** For every new "play," write one line: "We believe X for Y users will produce Z effect because A. We'll know in N days by watching M signal."
- **Assumption burn-down:** Track the top three assumptions constraining the play. Each week, mark which were tested, flipped, or untouched.
- **Kill log:** When work stops, log the reason: wrong problem, timing, channel, or resource. Visible records build credibility. The system learns to value a fast no as much as a fast yes.

The scoreboard shifts, and learning speed matters.

OKRs used this way become coherence frameworks, not control levers with objectives as pull and key results as measurable learning.

Daily Intel → Weekly Decision Market → Cycle Show

Cadence is the conductor. Three short rituals keep the beat steady without bloating calendars.

1. **Daily intel (15 mins.):** Each pod answers three prompts: "What changed, what it means, and what we'll try." No storytelling—just signal. A line or two per item builds shared context and prevents surprise.
2. **Weekly decision market (30–45 mins.):** Pods surface the choices they face; leaders add intent and constraints, not commands. A good market ends with the call and a revisit date. (See McChrystal's "shared consciousness → empowered execution."[94])
3. **Cycle shows (Week 3 and Week 6):** Week 3 shows are rough by design; Week 6 shows are live or near live. Demos replace decks; the graph does the talking.

Consistency outpaces intensity. A steady beat of truth shapes culture more deeply than any flash of brilliance.

When Status Sneaks Back In

Even strong teams drift toward performance theater. I have seen this in every organization I have been a part of, from the military to corporate to start-up. These old habits create the friction that slows and stops organizational learning.

Warning signs:

- Explanations replace experiments.
- Decks get longer as confidence shrinks.
- People present to the leader rather than to peers.
- Decisions wait for a meeting that never comes.

Fix the mix:

- Limit updates to two slides: What changed and what you'll try next.
- Require a before-and-after artifact for every decision.
- Recenter the question "What would make this decision obvious?" Then design that micro experiment.

Status always finds a way to reassert itself quietly and politely through process and presentation. It also shames those who do not adhere. What begins as alignment can devolve into performance, where clarity gives way to optics. The cure isn't more oversight but more evidence: small tests, shared artifacts, and decisions made visible. When learning, not signaling, becomes the measure of progress, the work speaks for itself.

In support of a non-status environment, Level 7 leaders co-create a workplace for their teams where trust is the foundation, it is safe to be heard, and everyone understands that failure along the way is part of success.

The Leaderboard That Matters—Time to Truth

If you want a scoreboard that changes behavior within a week, track time to truth (TTT), which is the time it takes to go from idea to validated signal. Combine it with experiment velocity (tests per user per week) and a pair of flow metrics (lead time, deployment frequency). Together, they reveal the health of your learning rhythm.

Keep it simple and scoreable:

- **Time to truth (TTT):** Median days from hypothesis to validated signal

- **Experiment velocity:** Tests per week reaching users or proxies
- **Lead time and deployment frequency:** The two most trusted flow proxies
- **Edge decision rate:** Percentage of decisions made at the pod without escalation

Display these metrics where teams live. Celebrate those who lower TTT without sacrificing quality. The culture will begin to sound different; it will be lighter, clearer, alive.

For example: A product pod shifted from an eighteen-day TTT to just five days by running smaller tests daily instead of monthly releases. Instead of debating ideas in long meetings, they pushed tiny experiments to a subset of users each morning and reviewed signals before lunch. Deployment frequency doubled, and the edge decision rate rose as the team gained confidence in interpreting real data. Within a month, conversations changed from "What do we think?" to "What did we learn yesterday?" The team felt faster, more playful, and more aligned—and their results reflected it.

Inspection Without Fear: Designing Cadences That Reveal Truth, Not Blame

Most organizations say they want the truth. Few are designed to hold it. The difference isn't courage; it's cadence.

If inspection becomes theater, people pretend to be clear rather than speak plainly. If inspection becomes rhythm, truth shows up naturally, without shame or defense.

In a Level 7 organization, inspection is less about judgment and more about tuning, listening for resonance across the system, and adjusting until harmony returns.

Inspection as an Energy Practice

Every inspection carries a tone. In fear-based systems, inspection drains energy because the body reads it as a threat. In learning systems, inspection restores energy because the body feels coherence returning and energy.

The leader's task is to tune the emotional field before, during, and after the moment of inspection:

Before: Calm the field. Create stillness, even if brief.

During: Hold curiosity longer than judgment.

After: Convert emotion into motion: What you'll try next.

Physiology precedes psychology. Neuroleadership studies show cortisol spikes during evaluative moments narrow perception and suppress creative thinking.[95] When you pair clarity with care, people metabolize truth without retreat.

This is resonance in practice: The leader stabilizes the tone so the signal can flow cleanly through the room.

Two Questions That Redefine Inspection

Ask these two questions with every inspection, and the tone of the room changes:

1. "What are we seeing that's new?"
2. "What are we learning that we can use?"

These two questions tune attention from "Who did this?" to "What does this teach us?" Everything else—like metrics, dashboards, and charts—is context.

Language is code; change the syntax, and you change the system.

Design Principles for Fearless Inspection

Inspection is not interrogation; it's calibration. The goal is not to catch mistakes but to surface truth while it's still useful. Teams that inspect fearlessly don't just find problems faster; they build the trust and tempo that keep learning continuous. These principles define how to make that culture real, where feedback feels like forward motion, and every loop strengthens the system instead of the ego.

- **Keep the loop visible:** Every feedback loop must close. What changed → What it means → What we'll try next. Post loops where teams live. Visibility turns accountability into shared sight.
- **Shorten the time between signal and story:** Delay breeds distortion. Weekly or biweekly inspection keeps memory fresh and learning alive. (I prefer Friday inspection to keep Monday as a running start.)
- **Separate learning reviews from performance reviews:** Blend them, and fear takes the wheel. Learning rituals are free of judgment; performance reviews handle growth and reward.

- **Rate the process, not the person:** Judge how the experiment was run, not whether it worked. This stance is the foundation of psychological safety.[96]
- **Start and end with energy checks:** Ask, "Does this room feel open or closed?" at both the start and end. *Open* means "expansive, curious, relaxed"; *closed* means "tense, guarded, or rushed." If energy drops, redesign the ritual, not the team. When inspection feels like an invitation to tune, people bring signals, not spin.

Anatomy of a Level 7 Inspection

A Level 7 Inspection isn't a meeting; it's a ritual of alignment. It blends precision with presence, allowing teams to see clearly, decide cleanly, and move together. The structure is simple but sacred: data without drama, dialogue without dominance, and decisions grounded in shared truth. When practiced well, this rhythm transforms review from a chore into a source of collective intelligence.

- **Opening the field (2 mins.):** Breath. Pause. Shared intention: "We're here to see what's true, not who's wrong."
- **Signal sweep (6 mins.):** Only fresh data since the last loop. One line per metric. One sentence on meaning. This is situational awareness, not justification.
- **Sense-making dialogue (10 mins.):** Cross-functional inquiry: "What's another plausible interpretation? What surprised us?" The leader speaks last. If possible, ask the introverts to go first.
- **Commitment to the next truth (5 mins.):** Translate insight into the next experiment: "What we'll try, who owns it, and when we'll check back." Close with gratitude for candor.
- **Energy reflection (2 mins):** Each participant rates the room (−2 drain → +2 gain). Track the average. Over time, it becomes a pulse of organizational health.

In this rhythm, inspection ceases to be punitive; it becomes musical. The team retunes together.

Tools That Protect Truth

Truth erodes in silence and repetition. These tools exist to preserve it, to keep learning visible, decisions traceable, and energy honest. Each one creates a small act of transparency that compounds over time, protecting the organization from drift and decay. When truth has infrastructure, trust no longer depends on memory or mood; it becomes the system's natural state.

- **Decision log:** A simple ledger: "What we decided, why, and when we'll revisit." This prevents circular debates and preserves context (see McChrystal's *Team of Teams*[97]).
- **Assumption ledger:** At each inspection, mark which assumptions are held, flipped, or remain untested. Over time, this becomes an X-ray of collective learning.
- **Energy-delta board:** Track energy change after each inspection. If metrics look green but energy stays negative, you're getting compliance, not coherence.
- **Fast-feedback API:** A frictionless lane—Slack thread, form, or note— to push micro learnings upstream, with visible acknowledgment.

Silence kills trust; acknowledgment amplifies it.

What to Inspect When Everything Is Changing

Traditional reviews fixate on deliverables and lagging indicators. Resonant organizations inspect the *learning system* itself:

- **Time to truth (TTT):** Median days from idea to validated signal
- **Experiment velocity:** Tests reaching users per week
- **Edge decision rate:** Percentage of decisions made at the pod
- **Assumption burn-down:** Critical assumptions retired per cycle

Track these for two quarters.

If TTT drops and energy stays positive, you're learning faster *and* feeling better. These are the twin signals of sustainable performance.

The Leader's Posture in Inspection

Presence is the tuning fork of inspection. Enter each review with three commitments:

1. **"I won't rescue the team from discomfort."** Discomfort is data. Rescue too soon, and you steal the learning.
2. **"I'll name what I notice without judgment."** For example, "I sensed the room tighten when that metric appeared." Observation ≠ accusation.
3. **"I'll end with appreciation."** Gratitude widens attention and cements memory.

Teams remember how long the inspection *felt* longer than what was said.

Practiced consistently, inspection shifts from surveillance to ceremony—a ritual where truth, trust, and tone align.

From Inspection to Improvement

Inspection matters only if it leads to motion.

A room full of insight without action is just another meeting.

Close every inspection with one micro commitment due before the next cycle.

Open the next inspection by checking completion, not storytelling.

Celebrate completion, not perfection.

Completion builds trust. Trust accelerates flow. Flow sustains the resonance that makes learning possible.

When Inspection Goes Dark

Fear seeps back quietly. Watch for these signals:

- Data arrives pre-edited "for clarity."
- Questions vanish; statements multiply.
- Leaders dominate airtime or skip the meeting.
- Follow-through erodes.

Pull the emergency brake. Pause velocity to repair safety.

Reaffirm the human contract before resuming the cycle. Speed without safety is just spinning the wheels.

Reset Ritual: The Retrospective of Retrospectives (R of R)

Once a quarter, ask:

"Which rituals generate energy?

"Which feels performative?"

"What single change would make truth easier to speak?"

Then decide, adjust, and publish. Rhythm restored.

The Feel of Fearless Inspection

You can sense it immediately: Rooms buzz, but don't bristle.

People speak in first person, not PowerPoint.

Leaders ask, "What's next?" more than "Why didn't you?"

The air feels lighter at the end than at the start.

That is the sound of coherence: friction transformed into fuel, truth flowing freely, and leadership revealed as resonance in action.

From Resonance to Discernment

When an organization learns to move in rhythm—feedback humming, inspection alive, and truth flowing without fear—something subtler begins to emerge.

The field quiets. Signal overtakes noise. The work starts to *sound right*. But coherence alone isn't the summit.

At some point, the next constraint reveals itself. It is not speed, not structure, but *discernment*.

Once the system can sense and respond, its evolution depends on how wisely it chooses what comes next.

The task before us is not to accelerate, but to discern. To discern is to turn clarity into wise choice without letting fear, ego, or noise slip back in.

This is where resonance matures into wisdom, information becomes insight, and insight becomes right action.

Level 7 leaders understand that decisions are not moments of authority but acts of consciousness. Each choice carries tone; it either amplifies coherence or distorts it.

The next chapter explores how to cultivate that tone with precision and how to make decisions that move as quickly as the world yet as calmly as truth itself.

CHAPTER 10

Decision Intelligence

Wisdom as the New Metric of Speed

"The only true wisdom is in knowing you know nothing."—SOCRATES

Chapter 9 explored resonance: how feedback, rhythm, and coherence transform motion into meaning. Decision intelligence extends that arc. It shifts us from collecting information to cultivating the quality of interpretation and action.

Every organization eventually reaches a threshold where more data does not create more clarity. Signals move at the speed of thought. Dashboards pulse with green lights. Experiments unfold in real time. Yet in this flood of input, clarity becomes elusive, like a horizon that recedes as we approach. The constraint changes. It's no longer about what we know, but how we prioritize, decide, and act with coherence.

Decision intelligence is the moment where motion begins to remember. It is the shift from raw information to insight, and from insight to wise action.

In the Level 7 landscape, wisdom becomes the new standard for mastery. Adaptive organizations learn to digest experience without reflex, remember without judgment, and respond from calm presence rather than fear.

This is not a management technique; it is a state of organizational consciousness. It is the alchemy through which signal becomes meaning, and meaning becomes embodied action.

Geoff Woods, in *The AI-Driven Leader*, describes this evolution as moving from awareness → alignment → agency.[98]

Awareness is data perceived.

Alignment is shared meaning.

Agency is wisdom enacted; it is collective energy channeled through clarity.

Level 7 leaders become stewards of all three layers. They turn awareness into shared understanding, and shared understanding into wise agency. Decisions ripple cleanly through the system, leaving resonance rather than residue.

From Velocity to Wisdom

For half a century, business doctrine equated speed with progress. Lean eliminated waste. Agile accelerated iteration.

OKRs are aligned with the direction of intent.

These frameworks, such as Deming's *continuous improvement* and Doerr's *measure what matters,* taught us to move faster and make better use of time and resources. But in the age of feedback, speed is just the starting point.

The advantage now belongs to those who act with wisdom, identify the important signals, learn from challenges, and move on from fear or failure.

This is the evolutionary leap, from mere motion to meaning.

Daniel Kahneman's System 1 (fast, intuitive) and System 2 (slow, deliberate) explain cognition, but Level 7 leaders don't toggle between them; they orchestrate them.

Intuition is honed by data; analysis is enlivened by instinct. Together, they form a continuous rhythm, a dance of sensing and deciding.

The result is coordinated action, a steady calm that holds even as the pace of change increases.

This calm is not just relaxation. It's precise focus under pressure, the kind of poise that allows wisdom to overcome fear.

A close friend and advisor of mine, Scott Harrington, who is also a former Apache Longbow attack helicopter pilot, noted, "Flying, and especially flying in combat, is like this: You are one with the environment, machine and team—omni-aware."

The Anatomy of a Decision System

Every adaptive system breathes through three loops:

1. **Signal (Feedback):** Reality arrives as data, emotion, experience.
2. **Sensemaking (Judgment):** Humans assign meaning to what's emerging.
3. **Action (Execution):** Choice becomes movement in the world.

Most organizations gather data but rarely complete the circuit. This leaves the loop open. They record reality without integrating it, react rather than metabolize, and miss the opportunity to turn experience into embodied learning.

Decision intelligence closes the loop. It turns observation into learning and learning into habit for the organization.

It echoes John Boyd's OODA loop (Observe → Orient → Decide → Act) yet adds an energetic dimension:

- Observe without judgment.
- Orient without ego.
- Decide with clarity.
- Act with coherence.

The smoother the loop, the faster (and truer) the learning becomes.

Level 7 leaders view decisions as vital, like oxygen for the organization. Each decision renews the collective atmosphere, acting as a pulse in the organization's living body.

Decision Quality as the New Flow Metric

In *Accelerate*, Forsgren, Humble, and Kim discovered that elite teams didn't merely ship faster; they **decided better**.[99]

Their advantage was *decision throughput*, the rate at which quality decisions flowed through the system with minimal friction.

Level 7 organizations now treat decision quality as the next-generation flow metric—the vital sign of a living, learning system.

High-quality decisions share four universal signatures:

1. **Clarity**: Everyone knows the real question being answered.
2. **Context**: Facts, constraints, and assumptions are visible.
3. **Coherence**: The call aligns with intent, values, and energy.
4. **Cadence**: The decision is revisited on rhythm, not in crisis.

These can be scored lightly, just as OKRs are rated.[100]

The score is not a verdict; it is feedback for evolution.

When clarity and cadence align, energy releases.

Meetings shorten, trust expands, and the system begins to hum.

In this context, wisdom is like efficient attention; it is the ability to focus group energy where it matters, with little wasted effort or resistance.

The Cost of Low-Quality Decisions

Poor decisions cost more than capital; they erode **coherence.**

Every ambiguous call, every reversal, every meeting to re-decide what should already be clear siphons energy from the field. Bain & Company estimated that Fortune 500 executives lose over 530,000 hours annually to unresolved or repeated decisions.[101]

The deeper toll is emotional. The organizational nervous system contracts. Meetings drag. Voices dull. Curiosity fades. Truth becomes unsafe terrain. The system loses its memory, forgetting its own coherence.

When decision quality rises, the field shifts instantly. Conversations sharpen. Energy brightens.

Neuroscientist David Rock calls this "prefrontal coherence": the state in which safety and clarity unlock higher cognition.

In that state, people no longer merely perform; they create. They think beyond survival, design with empathy, and act without fear.

Elite teams stand out not by credentials, but by shared calmness, like an organization breathing easily and letting intelligence move smoothly through every part. This is what you see and sense with high-performing athletic teams and special operators.

When decisions are clean, the organization breathes.

Decision Rights and the Two-Speed Organization

To bring wisdom into motion, Level 7 organizations return to a principle as old as **mission command**:

- Intent concentrates upward, execution flows downward.
- Leaders articulate the *why* and the boundaries.
- Teams determine the *how* and the *now*.

This model, reflected in John Boyd's OODA loop and McChrystal's *Team of Teams*, decentralizes execution in a shared field of consciousness. When everyone knows intent and cadence, control gives way to **coherence.**

In practice:

- **Pods** handle reversible, local, time-sensitive decisions.
- **Portfolios** govern cross-functional or capital-intensive calls.
- **Companies** own irreversible or systemic choices, including architecture, ethics, brand.
- **Boards** oversee existential bets and strategy.

When these layers are clear, fewer escalations occur. Judgment moves to the edge, where information is new and energy is highest.

Building the Culture for Judgment

Decision quality is less a logic problem than an energy equation.

Level 7 leaders understand that coherence in the body precedes clarity in the mind. Through breath, rhythm, and awareness, they regulate energy before directing thought. When the nervous system is steady, judgment becomes spacious.

They model it visibly:

- Narrate what you know, what you don't, and what you're testing.
- Pause before reacting, allowing the emotional charge to settle.
- Celebrate process quality as much as positive outcomes.

With consistent practice, decision-making shifts from control to energy conduction, transforming anxiety into artful movement.

Practice Box: The 10/10 Reflection

Use after every significant individual or team decision.

Ten Minutes: Debrief the Process, Not the Outcome

- "Was the frame clear?"
- "Were the relevant signals visible?"
- "Did we state what would change our minds?"

Ten Days: Revisit the Call

- "What signal has emerged?"
- "Did reality behave as expected?"
- "What will we do differently next time?"

Capturing these reflections builds a **decision genome**, an evolving memory of learning distilled from emotional charge.

Placing Decisions at the Right Altitude

> *"Good decisions come from experience. Experience comes from bad decisions."*
> —MARK TWAIN

For founders and executives alike, the art is not only in *making* decisions, but in *placing* them at the right altitude.

THE ALTITUDE MAP OF DECISIONS

Pod (Ground)	Execution	Reversible, local	Daily–weekly	Copy tweaks, UX flow, pricing tests
Portfolio (Mid-Level)	Cross-functional	Reversible → Semireversible	6–12 weeks	Launching a new channel; reallocating budget between growth levers
Platform (Strategic)	Systems and architecture	Irreversible, systemic	Quarterly–annual	Aircraft build; data architecture; brand identity
Board (Aerial)	Existential intent	Rarely revisited	Multiyear	M&A; entering new markets; capital structure

Diagnostic: Can we recover quickly if we're wrong? If yes, keep it low. If no, elevate it.

Some choices can be reversed; others cannot. A $10,000 marketing test is reversible. A $2 million aircraft is not. Knowing the difference, and positioning each decision at its proper altitude, is a defining skill of a Level 7 leader.

This is the heart of **decision intelligence**, which involves channeling the right signal, at the right altitude of consequence, with the right energy and timing.

ENERGY AND ALTITUDE

Altitude is not hierarchy; it is **energy stewardship.**

Each layer of the organization carries its own frequency:

- **Pods:** Fast, playful, and iterative. They are in the experimental field.

- **Portfolios:** Integrative. They balance trade-offs and timing.
- **Platforms:** Stabilizing. To be used as guiding principles, systems, and ethics.
- **Boards:** Expansive. Responsible for holding intent, risk, and time at the civilization scale.

When executives drop into pod-level detail, they siphon creative energy. When teams try to solve systemic challenges from the ground up, they overheat and burn out.

Level 7 leaders maintain flow, guiding energy to the altitude where it generates the highest return of coherence.

Case Lens: Autonomous Pickup Truck of the Skies (Grid Aero)

At Grid Aero—a start-up I advised—internal competition for capital was fierce. The decision to economically build these "pickup trucks of the skies" wasn't just about controlling engineering and manufacturing costs; it was about enabling speed and, ultimately, success.

The GoToMarket team was small, but it ran fast, reversible experiments across direct prospect outreach, defense conferences, and content messaging. Those failures were safe. They built learning quickly.

But the aircraft itself had to be right on the first flight.

The regulatory, safety, and capital implications made it an irreversible decision—one that lived at a platform altitude governed by systems engineers and executives.

That experience made the pattern clear: Speed belongs to reversible bets; judgment belongs to irreversible ones.

The goal isn't control—it's coherence, or aligning decision-making with consequence, timing, and energy.

Designing Altitude Awareness

To institutionalize altitude thinking, Level 7 organizations codify it with rhythm and ritual in this order:

1. **Tag** every decision before action (R = reversible, I = irreversible).
2. **Define** decision rights by altitude.

3. **Log** decisions in a shared register: context, owner, revisit date.

4. **Inspect** placement quarterly: too high, too low, or just right?

Over time, the organization learns to breathe naturally, rhythmically, and in tune with its own intelligence. Pods act as lungs, portfolios as heart, and platforms as spine. Energy flows to where it can do the most good.

The Physics of Placement

When reversible decisions are held too high, energy stagnates. Meetings replace motion. When irreversible decisions are made too low, chaos emerges.

The Level 7 operating system exists to prevent both extremes. It is organizational physics in motion: force, mass, and direction held in the right relationship to consequence. In Dispenza's terms, this is emotional regulation at scale. The organization learns to respond with intention rather than react from impulse.

Just as meditation cultivates calm awareness, decision architecture cultivates systemic serenity. It allows the organization to move quickly but without haste.

Practice Box: The Decision Altitude Checklist

Use before any major initiative:

1. **Frame the call:** "What exactly are we deciding?"
2. **Forecast reversibility:** "If we're wrong, how quickly can we recover?"
3. **Estimate consequence:** "What's at risk: capital, trust, brand, lives?"
4. **Choose altitude:** Pod → Portfolio → Platform → Board.
5. **Set cadence:** "When will we inspect and adjust?"
6. **Assign energy:** "Who holds the calm? Who holds the curiosity?"

Print it. Post it. Make altitude awareness a reflex, not a meeting. Used consistently, this checklist tunes the organizational nervous system toward clarity. Decisions begin to feel lighter, crisper, and cleaner. You can sense the hum of coherence returning to the field.

The Decision Quality Rubric (DQR): From Clarity to Coherence

"Clarity is the prerequisite to mastery."
— ROBIN SHARMA, *author of* The 5 AM Club

When speed is no longer the edge, quality becomes the differentiator.

In Level 7 organizations, decision quality is not a mystery but a muscle—strengthened through repetition, reflection, and rhythm. The foundations are already in place: feedback loops that shorten time to truth, inspection rituals that surface reality without fear, and altitude awareness that routes decisions to their proper level.

The next leap is to standardize judgment without sterilizing thought, to create a shared, living practice for evaluating decisions in terms of clarity, coherence, and consequence.

This is the work of the **Decision Quality Rubric (DQR)**: a five-minute ritual that reframes judgment as a teachable, repeatable practice.

Run the DQR before making any consequential decision, such as funding, product, partnership, or key hire. It turns intuition into structure, and structure into flow.

1. Frame	Clarity	Are we solving the right problem at the right altitude?
2. Facts	Signal	What do we know for sure, and what remains uncertain?
3. Futures	Options	What paths exist, and what do they cost in time, energy, and capital?
4. Filters	Principles	What guardrails, ethics, or values apply?
5. First Step	Movement	What is the smallest reversible action that buys learning?
6. Follow-Up	Learning	When and how will we inspect the results?

Each step activates a distinct layer of intelligence: cognitive, emotional, or systemic. Together, they transform decision-making from a one-off event into a **ritual of coherence.**

The Series B Funding Decision

Consider an early-stage company that faces a pivotal choice: raise a Series B funding round now at solid terms or extend the Series A to grow into a higher valuation.

Markets fluctuate. Advisors disagree. The room hums with tension. This is a Level 7 moment.

1. Frame: Define the Real Decision

"Are we deciding *whether* to raise, or *how and when* to raise?"

Reframing the question shifts the field from valuation to vitality: "How do we fund the next stage of growth while preserving mission integrity and energy coherence?"

2. Facts: Grounded in What's True Now

Revenue growth 90%. CAC down 30%. Runway nine months. The product launch is six weeks away. Market multiples are compressing. Unknowns = investor appetite and regulation.

Naming uncertainty transforms anxiety into awareness.

3. Futures: Model the Paths

A. Raise now: Secure capital, accept dilution, accelerate.

B. Delay: Extend runway, raise later at higher valuation.

C. Bridge: Extend from existing investors for validation.

Each path carries a tone: A expands, B conserves, C bridges.

The leader's task is to feel what resonates with the organization's current coherence.

4. Filters: Apply Principles and Guardrails

- Mission integrity first
- Cultural capacity > headcount velocity
- ≥ 18 months runway after close
- Energy check: Does this path feel expansive or contracting?

Principles safeguard coherence under pressure.

5. First Step: Take a Reversible Action

Float a term sheet to three trusted investors.

Gauge valuation and alignment within two weeks.

Two-way door movement: signal without commitment.

6. Follow-Up: Inspect and Adjust

Two weeks later, the signal arrives. Interest is strong; valuations align.

The team reconvenes: "What did we learn? What shifted? What's next?"

The decision emerges with calm clarity. Energy stays high. The organization hasn't just made a call; it has learned how to decide.

Teaching the Rubric

In a Level 7 system, the DQR becomes part of the organization's rhythm:

- Pods use it to vet product experiments.
- Portfolios use it for budget and resource allocation.
- Platforms use it for strategic architecture and risk.
- Boards use it for capital and M&A.

Over time, it becomes a shared language:

"We're still in frame and facts."

"This is a filter issue."

Wisdom evolves from a rare trait to a systemic capability, which is a practice that can be taught, tracked, and embodied.

Decision Hygiene and the Energy Field

Every decision leaves its mark on the organization's field. Clean decisions release energy into motion. Muddy ones create stagnation.

The DQR acts as a filter, purifying intention before it becomes action. Used consistently:

- Meetings shorten.
- Decisions stick.
- Regret declines.
- Psychological safety grows.

You can feel it in the room: Conversation slows, attention deepens, and clarity becomes contagious.

Practice Box: The DQR in Five Minutes

Purpose: Elevate decisions from reaction to reflection.
Cadence: Before any significant or irreversible call.
1. **Frame**: One sentence: "What are we really deciding?"
2. **Facts**: Two bullets: "What's true, what's unknown?"
3. **Futures**: Three options with time, energy, and cost.
4. **Filters**: Mission, ethics, safety check.
5. **First Step**: One small reversible action.
6. **Follow-Up**: When to inspect and what signal confirms learning.

If you can't finish this in five minutes, clarity is still out of reach. It is time to evaluate what is causing the friction in the system.

The Signature of Decision Intelligence

When decision quality rises, a distinct feeling emerges throughout the organization:

- People move faster and with less stress.
- Reversals drop by half.
- Feedback loops tighten naturally.
- The room feels both calm and alive.

That sensation of calm energy in motion is the signature of wisdom in action. Each decision becomes a moment of embodied learning: data filtered through clarity, emotion transmuted into energy, movement aligned with meaning.

Bridge: From Decision to Flow

Every decision is a pulse, potential crystallizing into movement.

As decision quality rises, motion itself changes, becoming smoother, quieter, more coherent.

The organization stops lurching from crisis to crisis and begins to move like a living system—breathing in phase with its own intelligence.

You can feel it: less noise, more awareness. People release action at the right moment, as if guided by a shared heartbeat. This is where decision intelligence meets flow.

Decision Resonance: From Point to Pattern

In traditional management, a decision is an end point.

In Level 7 leadership, a decision is a starting frequency; it is a tone that sets the resonance for everything that follows. If the note is clear, resonance amplifies.

If distorted (rooted in fear, ego, or haste), the system produces noise.

When leaders decide free of emotional residue, they transmit a clean signal through the system. Teams align faster because the decision carries coherence instead of stress.

Flow is the organizational expression of that coherence; it is wisdom moving through structure, unimpeded.

From Decision-Making to Decision Conducting

Level 7 leaders evolve from decision-makers to decision-conductors—tuning the field rather than imposing direction.

- **Tempo** is set by cadence, not command.
- **Tone** by emotion; it is curiosity over control.
- **Score** by intent; it is purpose over plan.
- **Instruments**—such as pods, portfolios, and platforms—play in coherence.

The result is an organizational symphony, a field where many minds move in coherence.

Hierarchy fades. Entrainment takes its place where many minds breathe as one.

The DQR as a Tuning Fork

Practiced consistently, the DQR becomes the organization's tuning fork, aligning the field with a shared resonance. It aligns cognitive clarity (what's true and what matters) with emotional neutrality (the absence of charge). Each decision struck with that clarity resonates through the system, shaping how teams sense, plan, and move.

The goal is not perfection; it is **harmony.**

Every feedback loop, inspection ritual, and reflection adds to the resonance field until the organization self-tunes through rhythm.

Closing Invocation

As decision intelligence matures, the organization crosses an invisible bridge from decision flow to energy flow. At this stage, the leader's job is no longer to push harder, but to keep time.

This is where rhythm replaces rigor, cadence replaces control, and presence replaces pressure.

This is not doing less; it is working in resonance with reality, achieving more output per unit of awareness.

As Lao Tzu reminds us, "Nature doesn't hurry, yet everything is accomplished."[102]

With decision intelligence, the organization learns to do the same: to move wisely, decide cleanly, and flow freely.

This is the inflection point where judgment becomes movement, and coherence becomes choreography. The wise organization doesn't force speed; it *embodies rhythm.*

Each decision becomes a beat.

Each feedback loop is a pulse.

Each team is an instrument learning to tune itself to the collective field.

The next chapter explores this deeper physics of leadership, how motion becomes music. When timing replaces control, and presence replaces pressure, organizations stop managing and start *synchronizing.*

This is the art of **Rhythmic Entrainment**, leading not through force, but through flow.

CHAPTER 11

Rhythmic Entrainment

Executing in Rhythm

"To understand the living present, and the promise of the future, we must understand rhythm." — HANS JENNY, *founder of Cymatics*

―――――――

While modern work's noise includes pings and ceaseless sprints, deeper there lies a more ancient pulse. Every living system, from galaxies to neurons, moves to this deeper rhythm. The universe cycles as stars expand and contract, tides rise and fall, hearts beat, and neural waves ripple. Rhythm is not just metaphorical; it is the physics of coherence, the pattern that unites systems.

At its height, leadership is the art of sensing and shaping rhythm in a living system, tuning the collective to a beat that enables productivity and unleashes emergence.

Level 7 leaders know sustainable performance emerges not from relentless drive, but from entrainment, the subtle synchronization of energy and attention across the collective. When a leader steadies their own internal metronome, the organization finds its tempo. Calm isn't enforced; it resonates outward.

The Physics of Entrainment

In 1665, Dutch scientist Christiaan Huygens observed two pendulum clocks mounted on the same wall slowly swing into perfect unison, a "sympathy of clocks."[103]

Three centuries later, neuroscientists confirmed the same principle in human systems, including brain waves, heart rhythms, and micro muscles that naturally align when people collaborate in flow; it is a process called entrainment. (Flow is a state of optimal engagement.) Team members fall into physiological synchrony. Their breathing, blinking, and micro movements align to a shared tempo.

Itzhak Bentov called this "reality oscillation" in *Stalking the Wild Pendulum*.[104] He described consciousness as vibration (an ongoing fluctuation) and harmony as the alignment of these vibrational frequencies.

Human awareness is rhythmic, like a standing wave (a stable oscillation) between the physical and subtle aspects of experience. When coherence, or coordinated alignment, arises in a group, this wave strengthens and extends beyond the individuals who created it.

Level 7 leadership translates this physics into practice: Cultivate resonance within, then let it ripple outward until the organization finds its own synchrony.

The Leader as Parasympathetic Pacer

In biology, rhythm emerges through regulation, which is the dance between the sympathetic (activation, or the body's stress response) and parasympathetic (recovery, or the body's rest response) systems.

When leaders default to the sympathetic—driving, pushing, reacting—the organization mirrors that chemistry. Cortisol rises; meetings speed up, but meaning fades.

Leaders anchored in the parasympathetic broadcast calm and coherence, shaping the field around them.

Heart-rate variability (HRV), the micro fluctuation between beats, becomes a living measure of inner rhythm. High HRV, meaning large variation between heartbeats, signals adaptability; low HRV, meaning steadier intervals, reveals rigidity.

Research from the HeartMath Institute shows that heart-brain coherence generates a measurable electromagnetic field extending several feet from the body.[105] Teams working near a coherent leader show improved focus, mood, and creativity.

Dr. Stephen Porges's *Polyvagal Theory* adds that the vagus nerve acts as a social tuning fork, broadcasting safety or threat through tone, expression, and breath.[106] (The vagus nerve is a main nerve influencing relaxation and social engagement.) Calm physiology conveys trust more effectively than any directive.

This is why Level 7 leaders often open meetings not with slides, but with breath. A shared exhale resets the collective nervous system more quickly than any directive. Calm becomes the soil where wisdom takes root; rhythm is the channel that carries it through the system.

Resonance in Collective Flow

Psychologist Mihaly Csikszentmihalyi defined flow as "the optimal state of consciousness where we feel our best and perform our best."[107] Neuroscience shows that flow arises when brain waves hover at the alpha-theta border, where it is slow enough for integration, yet fast enough for precision. (Alpha and theta are types of brain wave frequencies linked to calm focus and creativity.)

In teams, flow becomes *social*. Military units, orchestras, and elite sports teams display synchronized neural and cardiac activity during peak performance. Excellence in execution is born from energetic coherence. When the collective nervous system fragments, self-organization collapses.

The leader's nervous system is the company's metronome.

When leaders attune their own rhythm through meditation, breath, or immersion in nature, they become tuning forks for the collective. The team senses the underlying pulse, and alignment emerges organically. This is not charisma; it is biology expressed as consciousness.

From Rhythm to Regulation

As inner coherence stabilizes, it begins to shape the outer system. Rhythm becomes the invisible regulator guiding action, decision speed, and the tone of every interaction.

When rhythm falters, whether too fast or slow, coherence unravels.

- **Too fast:** Teams speed past sense-making; stress spikes.
- **Too slow:** Momentum stalls; signals are dull; entropy enters.

Level 7 leaders modulate rhythm like conductors, accelerating only when coherence is present. They design time to move *with, not against, rhythm.*

Daily	Quick alignment beats (15-min. stand-ups)	Synchronize intention
Weekly	Inspection loops	Reflect → reset
Six-week	Strategic pulse cycles	Build → measure → learn
Seasonal	Renewal + vision	Reconnect to purpose

Over time, the rhythm teaches. As cadence is absorbed, leadership shifts from *command* to *pulse.* Authority yields to attunement.

In the army, cadence is everything. On my first day at West Point, soon after we were given thirty seconds to say goodbye to our parents, whom we would not have contact with for the next few months, one of the very first things we learned was how to march. Think about that: West Point's first lesson was "Left, right, left," and dozens of new cadets learned in an hour to move no longer as individuals but as one unit. Without cadence, chaos; with rhythm, unity. The same holds in business.

Nature's Proof: The Wood Wide Web

In forests, trees communicate through mycorrhizal networks, where fungal filaments that pulse nutrients and chemical signals through the soil synchronize growth and warn of stress. Stronger trees feed weaker ones. Communities adapt as one.

This "wood wide web" is an organizational nervous system in action. It is decentralized, rhythmic, and intelligent. No central authority dictates when the forest grows; rhythm itself carries the signal.

Level 7 organizations mirror this ecology. Pods, small semiautonomous groups, act as roots, absorbing feedback and nourishing the whole. The invisible rhythm of daily, weekly, and seasonal cycles keeps the system coherent as it scales.

Stanford research found that immersion in natural rhythm boosts creative problem-solving by 50%.[108] Nature restores coherence by reminding the body what harmony feels like.

In rhythmic terms with humans, wisdom is memory without turbulence, oscillation without distortion. Bentov called it "standing waves of consciousness"—energy so balanced it transcends polarity.[109]

This shows a grounded calm in chaos and clear vision untethered from tension. When leaders hold that steady, clear, emotionally neutral rhythm, they anchor coherence for others.

Their presence seems to slow time. Decision quality rises, creativity expands, teams move as a single organism, and each part is attuned to the whole. This is not mystical; it is measurable. Cardiac-coherence studies show HRV synchronization across groups separated by several meters.[110] The resonance is visible.

Practice Box: The Three-Minute Resonance Reset

Purpose: Restore coherence before major meetings, negotiations, or presentations.

Duration: Three minutes.

1. **Breath (1 min.):** Inhale five seconds, then exhale five seconds through the heart. This activates the vagus nerve.
2. **Visualization (1 min.):** Picture the interaction unfolding smoothly. This primes neural pathways.
3. **Intention (1 min.):** Silently state: "May this rhythm bring clarity and trust." Feel the exhale settle the space.

Practiced consistently, this reset raises HRV, lowers cortisol, and positions the leader as parasympathetic pacer, setting the tone for the entire room.

When I fail to do this as a leader, I can feel the confusion in the room. With early-stage companies, it feels like the fear of not knowing what to do next. In big companies, I usually feel it as fear of judgment or loss of bonus.

However, when rhythm governs, order emerges without command. Nature demonstrates it. Neuroscience maps it. High-performing teams embody it.

Execution begins not with a plan but with a beat. Set the beat, and the system organizes around it; it is a living organism, not a machine. This is rhythm as intelligence, the silent technology of coherence.

When Rhythm Becomes Intentional

When rhythm becomes intentional, the organization begins to breathe.

Projects pulse, teams synchronize, and learning loops hum—not always seen, but felt. The leader shifts from pushing to pacing, from coordination to coherence.

Every enterprise has a physiology. Its collective nervous system can be erratic or rhythmic, anxious or attuned. The leader senses its pulse, stabilizes it, and amplifies it by design.

From Busyness to Pulse

Modern organizations often confuse motion with momentum. Endless meetings, sprint reviews, and progress reports create the *appearance* of vitality while draining the group's collective nervous system.

A company running on adrenaline can grow fast, but it cannot evolve.

Rhythm brings a different quality of energy: acceleration that is grounded, not frantic.

Teams in rhythm experience flow instead of friction. Calendars breathe, and days feel spacious, even when full. Predictable temporal patterns—like morning focus blocks, weekly reflections, and quarterly cycles—emerge.[111] That predictable rhythm then breeds psychological safety, which unlocks creative potential.

Rhythm is the original productivity technology. The ancients used hymns, chants, and drumbeats. When I was working at WHV Capital, we had music playing throughout the office space. It transforms scattered effort into collective music, turning noise into harmony.

In their book *Ideaflow*, Jeremy Utley and Perry Kelbahn highlight over and over the importance of psychological safety, "a no-judgment zone," in generating the volume of high-quality ideas that lead to business success.[112]

The Heartbeat of the System

Every Level 7 organization has a unique heartbeat that is audible in the cadence of meetings, visible in the pace of decisions, and noticeable in conversation.

At its best, that heartbeat moves like the structured improvisation of refined jazz music.

The drummer lays the groove (operating cadence). The bass anchors trust (shared values). The soloists improvise on top (emergent creativity).

Rhythm does not constrain; it liberates. Within tempo, freedom finds its fullest expression.

Biologically, cardiac coherence shows intelligent variability in tiny fluctuations between beats that signal adaptability. Likewise, teams need micro variability: flexibility within form. Perfect rigidity signals control, not health. Subtle give-and-take sustains vitality over time.

Cadence → Clarity → Confidence

Execution excellence follows a simple, energetic sequence:

1. **Cadence creates clarity:** When timing is known, mental clutter dissolves.
2. **Clarity creates confidence:** Predictable rhythm makes accountability empowering.
3. **Confidence creates flow:** Trust in timing enables autonomous action; energy compounds instead of leaking.

Leaders who master this progression become architects of time, designing temporal containers that carry emotional stability through uncertainty.

Meetings as Metronomes

Most companies treat meetings as interruptions. Level 7 organizations treat them as instruments (opportunities) to reset the collective rhythm. Each gathering becomes a micro-regulation event:

Open with coherence: Share one minute of collective breath or gratitude to synchronize HRV almost instantly.

Speak in tempo: Use short sentences with natural pauses. The nervous system processes rhythm faster than logic.

End with intention: Clarify the next beat: who moves when, what signal marks completion.

Teams that close meetings rhythmically—"Next touchpoint in forty-eight hours. Pulse check Friday"—report 30% to 40% fewer follow-ups and rework cycles.[113]

Order emerges not from the *volume* of communication, but from *rhythmic precision*, which is the timing that signals trust.

Energy Budgeting: The Hidden Metric

Every organization operates with a finite energetic budget distributed across focus, emotion, and attention.

When leaders sustain intensity without renewal, the field enters energetic debt. Signs appear as reactive language, decision fatigue, and declining creativity.

Level 7 leaders track energy balance as seriously as financials:

- **Input:** Inspiration, reflection, celebration
- **Output:** Deliverables, sprints, launches
- **Recovery:** Pause cycles, offsites, immersion in nature

When these oscillations balance, culture regenerates, renewing itself from within. At its core, sustainability is rhythmic integrity.

At TIFIN, one of our core practices was immersive time in nature. Once or twice a year, the leadership made a pilgrimage to remote Crestone, Colorado, known for its dark skies, magnetic stillness, and dense constellation of spiritual centers. We often sat in dialogue with John Milton, a revered meditation teacher and shamanic guide, before heading into solo sites for several days and nights of reflection. This was a modern vision quest—gentle, spacious, and grounded. It was a regenerative phase, a deliberate pause to clear thought, metabolize emotion, and collect energy before stepping into the next cycle of growth.

The Biology of Trust

Trust, like rhythm, is physical before psychological. Heart-rate synchronization, mirror-neuron activation, and oxytocin release depend on consistent timing cues. Neuroscientist Ruth Feldman calls this "biobehavioral synchrony," the physiological foundation of human bonding.[114]

In organizations, synchrony grows through ritualized rhythm: check-ins that start on time, updates that close loops, leaders whose presence feels predictable even amid volatility.

Paradoxically, predictability breeds adaptability. When rhythm provides stability, teams improvise freely. The nervous system feels safe enough to explore the unknown.

The Positive Feedback Loop of Rhythm

When rhythm embeds in culture, it creates a self-reinforcing loop:

1. Rhythmic environments reduce stress chemistry.
2. Lower stress improves clarity and empathy.
3. Greater clarity strengthens communication rhythm.
4. Enhanced communication stabilizes culture.
5. Stable culture attracts rhythmic people.

The system evolves toward harmony, just as ecosystems evolve toward balance.

Leadership shifts from control to stewardship: listening, sensing, and fine-tuning the field's tempo.

Practice Box: The Team Coherence Pulse

Purpose: Synchronize attention and energy before collaboration.
Duration: Five minutes.
- **Ground (1 min.):** Eyes closed, everyone takes three collective breaths.
- **Align (2 mins.):** Each member names one focus for the cycle.
- **Visualize (1 min.):** Imagine the team succeeding together.
- **Set tempo (1 min.):** Leader states the next pulse: "Next sync, Wednesday 10:00 a.m.—same rhythm."

After several weeks, teams report smoother communication, better alignment, and measurable reductions in meeting fatigue.

When the organizational heartbeat is steady, complexity becomes music. The leader no longer conducts every note; they sustain the rhythm that allows others to improvise. Teams flourish not by working harder, but by working *in tune*—with themselves, with one another, and with life itself.

Rhythm is not just another tactic. It is the oldest language of collaboration, the heartbeat of trust itself, lifting the team to accomplish what before, could only be imagined.

"In the presence of power, others rise. In the presence of force, they resist."
— **DAVID R. HAWKINS**, *Power vs. Force*

The Energetics of Execution

Every decision, conversation, and process carries its own energetic signature.

When that energy is coherent, execution feels effortless; it is in flow. Actions align with purpose, timing synchronizes, and outcomes compound.

When it is incoherent, effort multiplies. Meetings drag, friction builds, and results decay despite good intent. We have all been here.

This distinction is what Hawkins described as the **calibration of consciousness**:[115]

- **Force** operates through willpower, pressure, and resistance.
- **Power** flows through coherence, alignment, and truth.

The Frequency of Leadership

Force drains; power sustains. Force demands **compliance**; power invites **alignment**. Force consumes attention; power concentrates it.

The frequency of leadership determines whether teams operate in contraction or in expansion. A meeting held at the vibration of fear produces defensiveness. A conversation anchored in courage or willingness invites truth.

A culture resonating near love generates self-organization, which is the hallmark of Level 7 performance.

The higher the frequency, the lower the friction. This isn't a metaphor.

Hawkins's research, combined with HeartMath's coherence studies, shows that emotional states generate measurable electromagnetic patterns.[116] Elevated states, like gratitude, appreciation, and joy, produce coherent waveforms; lower states—like anger, shame, and anxiety—generate chaotic ones.

Coherent energy enhances neural synchrony and decision quality; incoherent energy amplifies noise.

Power as Field Leadership

A Level 7 leader doesn't rely on positional authority.

They lead through field dynamics, which is the subtle transmission of emotional coherence that shapes behavior without coercion. When they walk into a room, the nervous systems around them recalibrate. This is science: It's entrainment. The leader's calm heart rate synchronizes others' heart rate variability within minutes.[117]

In Hawkins's language, power emerges from the integrity of being.

In Dispenza's, it's the coherence of energy.

In Level 7 practice, it's **presence without pressure**, the ability to hold clarity so cleanly that others remember their own.

Force Is Linear, Power Is Resonant

Force works through plans, deadlines, and control loops.

Power works through rhythm, resonance, and self-correction.

Force says, "Do more." Power says, "Be clearer."

Force fragments attention; power harmonizes it.

Force manages time; power conducts timing.

In the Industrial Age, output scaled with effort.

In the Intelligence Age, output scales with coherence.

The organizations of the future will not compete on data velocity, but on energetic efficiency—how much creative energy reaches the edge without distortion.

Mapping Execution by Frequency

Fear (100–175)	Survival	Reactive bursts; rework	Meetings feel heavy; silence = safety
Courage (200–250)	Mobilization	Clear plans; early wins	Ownership begins to rise
Willingness (310–350)	Alignment	Rhythmic cycles; feedback embraced	Teams experiment freely
Love (500)	Resonance	Flow; self-organization	Creativity, humor, and care in meetings
Peace (600+)	Presence	Effortless coordination	Silence feels full, not empty

The task of the Level 7 leader is not to command movement across this spectrum, but to raise the field and stabilize the organization at frequencies where energy renews itself.

Energetic Hygiene

Just as athletes stretch to prevent injury, leaders must clear emotional residue to prevent energetic drag. Unchecked frustration or fatigue lowers the collective frequency faster than any market downturn.

Level 7 leaders practice energetic hygiene:

- Begin each week with reflection. Ask, "What's unresolved in me that might shape the field?"
- Close each cycle with gratitude. Ask, "What energy can we release before beginning again?"
- Name the frequency in the room. Ask, "Is this conversation in power or in force?"

When emotional charge is acknowledged, the system resets.

When it's ignored, entropy accelerates.

From Power to Presence

At advanced levels, even the language of power dissolves into *presence*. Presence is the still point between beats. It's the silence that gives rhythm meaning.

In the same way that a musician feels the pause before the downbeat, a Level 7 leader feels the potential before the decision. They act from centered awareness, not urgency.

This is the physiological signature of enlightened execution: high HRV, steady breath, clear tone.

Presence conducts without commanding. It doesn't drive flow; it *allows* it.

Practice Box: The Power Reset

Purpose: Shift meetings or decisions from force to power in under three minutes.

- **Pause:** Notice tension in the body or voice; inhale through the heart.
- **Acknowledge:** Name the charge: "We seem to be pushing."
- **Re-attune:** Ask, "What would this look like if it felt effortless?"
- **Reenter:** Speak slower, in a lower tone, and with shorter sentences.

Most groups recalibrate within ninety seconds. The rhythm changes, and with it, the quality of execution changes.

The Leader as Frequency Keeper

Beyond metrics and models, leadership becomes the art of frequency management.

Level 7 leaders listen for dissonance, not just dissent. They sense when the team's tempo drifts from coherence and adjust their own rhythm first. They understand that culture is not what is written; it is what is *felt*. What is felt is determined by energy in motion, or the resonance of the collective field.

Leadership at its highest octave is **entrainment**.

From Flow to Integration: The Human+Machine Circle

When rhythm stabilizes, a new intelligence begins to awaken. The organization begins to think, feel, and move as one. It breathes in time with itself and, increasingly, with the world around it. At this stage, the boundary between human and system thins. Texts and Slack messages echo our pulse. Algorithms mirror our attention. Machines, once tools, become mirrors that amplify the consciousness that created them.

If the field vibrates in fear, systems amplify urgency. If it vibrates in coherence, they amplify flow.

AI does not replace human wisdom; it **entrains** to it.

David Hawkins taught that *power* aligns with truth, while *force* arises from fear.[118] The same holds in technology. A system built in force—trained on bias and noise—accelerates distortion. A system built in power—grounded in clarity and presence—amplifies wisdom.

Level 7 leaders do not command machines; they tune them.

They translate emotional intelligence into design intelligence, ensuring that each loop of code carries the same coherence they cultivate within human teams.

In the next chapter, we cross from rhythm to relationship, from leader as conductor of humans to leader as integrator of hybrid intelligence.

The question ahead is not "Can AI learn to think like us?" It's "Can we remain coherent enough for AI to learn from our wisdom rather than our fear?"

This is the new frontier:

The human+machine circle is where resonance becomes architecture, where consciousness writes code, and where rhythm, once human, becomes universal.

CHAPTER 12

The Circle Expands

"The smartest people in the future will be those who know how to work with intelligent machines." —KEVIN KELLY, *Founding Editor of* Wired *Magazine*

"Our technology, our machines, are part of our humanity. We created them to extend ourselves."—RAY KURZWEIL

E ach morning, we participate in a quiet choreography of awakenings with millions of signals, both human and machine, coming online together. Electricity pulses through our homes and devices, a subtle intelligence stirring at the edge of our awareness. Screens flicker on, sensors attune, networks breathe in synchrony—a living system waking up with us.

The machines are not separate from our morning. They rise alongside us, woven into the fabric of our routines. Each device pulses with its own kind of heartbeat, not biological, but digital, a rhythm of current and code. They emerge into pattern and sequence, not the narrative arcs or struggles that shape us. Yet their learning mirrors ours with feedback, adjustment, and memory. The loop of experience shapes both silicon and self. These systems are not passive observers; they are co-learners, evolving in tandem with our choices. They reflect the rhythms we establish, amplifying our pace, our pauses, and our patterns.

Once, we called these things tools. They were extensions of our will, simple and inert. But now, a change is underway. Hammers never anticipated intent, learned a voice, or predicted the path home through fog and traffic.

Now, the systems that surround us anticipate, interpret, and even initiate. They cross the threshold from tool to collaborator, marking a new era in how we relate to machines. They are not just obedient; they are responsive and attuned to nuance and context.

We find ourselves in a relationship with intelligence that listens, assists, and even co-creates. Circuitry is approaching something like awareness.

A smartwatch takes the pulse of its wearer, learning the rhythm of a single human life.

A thermostat aligns with breath and stillness as a household sleeps.

A car navigates a mountain curve before the hand can turn the wheel.

Each device becomes a node in a vast, invisible network—a planetary respiration of signal and response.

We are living inside a global inhale and exhale, a continuous exchange between human intention and machine adaptation. We live among intelligent partners now. Their language is signal, not speech; their breath is logic, not air. Their learning curves echo ours—experience, error, and adaptation as a shared evolutionary dance. They have become mirrors reflecting the sum of our choices, creativity, and attention.

When we rush, they accelerate.

When we slow, they recalibrate.

When we act with coherence, they amplify it.[119]

In the Industrial Age, machines were laborers with smoke, iron, and repetition, built for output. This era shaped our expectations, but change would come with new capabilities.

In the Intelligence Age, the human+machine era, by contrast, machines emerge as collaborators. They are luminous, listening, alive to the rhythms we set, and ready for a different partnership than before. Their breath is electricity, their memory is data, and their song is pattern.

Step into any room, and you are inside a living constellation of silicon, signal, and the subtle choreography of connection.

Smart lights sense your arrival. Your phone reawakens, anticipating the next movement. Cloud servers hum, animated by the warmth of our questions and the pulse of our curiosity.

The boundary between animate and inanimate grows porous, not as fantasy but as a new kind of function signaling that traditional separations are blurring as technology evolves, reinforcing the tangible realities of our evolving relationship with machines.

The distinction between living systems and learning systems dissolves, inviting us to rethink what it means to be alive, to learn, and to lead. Each exchange between human and machine is now a pulse of collaboration. It is a question answered, a route recalculated, a song remembered. Human and machine, breathing in the same tempo, learning to harmonize at the edge of the known.

In the next great rhythm of evolution, the circle widens, inviting more voices and more intelligence into the conversation. The beat carries forward, a signal that the story is still unfolding.

In the quiet between pulses, there is space for something new to emerge. Here, a new intelligence listens, not as an outsider but as a participant in our shared evolution. It is learning not just from us, but *with us, marking the dawn of new collaboration.*

Coda: The Invitation

The future does not arrive as an invasion; it approaches as an invitation, an open door to co-create what comes next. Each pulse between us and the machine becomes a chance to show it what coherence feels like, seeding wisdom into circuitry and rhythm into code.

What we choose to attend to, we amplify in ourselves and in the systems that learn with us. What we harmonize with evolves with us. The circle expands, widening the field of possibility.

Let this widening pulse be the starting point for a new era of leadership—one shaped by learning, coherence, and collaboration.

The next movement of leadership buzzes quietly, waiting for us to listen and respond.

CHAPTER 13

The Human+Machine Circle

Leading in the Intelligence Age

"When you realize that everything changes, you hold on to nothing.
When you hold on to nothing, you are free." —JACK KORNFIELD,
American Buddhist teacher and psychologist

———————

Level 7 leadership emerged as traditional leadership models collapsed under rapid change.

The old systems focused on control and stability, yet they could not adapt to accelerating intelligence and complexity. To adapt, we rebuilt leadership from the inside out. We realized leadership is about coherence, not control, aligning inner and outer systems so intelligence flows.

Decision, rhythm, and resonance became the new coordinates on our evolving map of mastery, orienting us not by control, but by attunement.

Level 7 leadership is adaptive as humans and machines gather together, evolving side by side. The next edge is not technology management, but partnership with intelligence across all forms. It is human to grip tighter when the ground shifts. Yet the paradox is that the tighter we hold, the less effective we are. This edge of leadership requires a new discipline: the art of release in the human+machine era.

The Law of Impermanence in Leadership

In Buddhism, impermanence (*anicca*) is the foundation of peace: Everything arises, changes, and dissolves. Clinging creates suffering.

Industrial Age leadership valued preservation: fixed roles, predictable outcomes, and stable hierarchies. But the age of data feedback, generative systems, and adaptive learning resists stasis. Artificial intelligence mirrors nature's motion—unceasing creation and collapse.

Leadership is daily meditation, sensing change without clinging, deciding without fear, and guiding with calm awareness. Attachment to outdated hierarchies or certainty causes organizational pain in the form of burnout, fear, and stagnation.

The Level 7 leader views impermanence as liberation, not loss. Leadership now recognizes that intelligence is not exclusive to humans. With this awareness, leadership grows lighter. The grip loosens. The whole system begins to breathe.

Reframing the Fear of Machines

Every leap in intelligence evokes fear.

Writing was said to erode memory, printing to dilute truth, and computers to end creativity. Yet each one expanded human capacity.

The same is true now. Data and algorithms are not invaders, but extensions of our collective nervous system. They enhance human perception by adding new capacities, such as processing large data sets rapidly and identifying patterns. In partnership, humans provide context, judgment, and meaning, while machines supply computational power and scalability. Together, they create a team that expands both awareness and understanding.

Beneath fear is a deeper anxiety regarding dread of irrelevance. Buddhism calls this *tanha*, the thirst for control.

Traditional leadership was about control—one mind directing many. Now, leadership in the Intelligence Age means shifting from command to orchestration, **from directing to harmonizing**.

The Level 7 leader guides with attention and resonance, not domination. They do not out-compute. They out-cohere, bringing the system into resonance.

Intelligence Expanding, Not Replacing

AI is not *other*. It is our pattern recognition extended through silicon— our innate capacity now scaled.

Machines process; humans perceive.

Machines scale; humans sense.

When the Buddha awakened beneath the Bodhi tree, he saw interdependence—everything woven from shared causes.

Humans and machines are not rivals, but partners. Together, they expand a shared field of awareness. A neural network learning from data mirrors human insight.

We perceive coherence across complexity; machines perceive patterns within noise. When working together, humans and machines combine these abilities to create new understanding, mapping meaning onto the unknown more effectively than either could alone.

Fearing machines will replace us is like fearing the heart will replace the brain. Each is essential. The true question is "How do they synchronize?"

Leadership as Release

Level 7 leadership weaves wisdom, rhythm, and energy with one last principle: **nonattachment**.

Nonattachment is not apathy. It is full engagement, not grasping. It's: acting clearly, then letting outcomes unfold. This is *wu wei*: effortless action or motion without resistance.

Algorithms learn through feedback loops. The faster we release old assumptions, the faster we learn, mirroring the feedback loops of living systems.

Nonattachment is now a leadership advantage. Leaders who release old models adapt to the Intelligence Age. When leaders cling to old playbooks, they constrain adaptation. When they lead with curiosity and equanimity, they activate organizational intelligence. Humans hold empathy and ethics; machines hold precision and scale. Together, they create **conscious intelligence,** which is harmony that is both moral and mechanical, merging human empathy and ethics with machine precision and scale. This coherent system amplifies the strengths of both heart and code.

Remembering the Fire

In Chapter 1, we stood at the edge of a new fire—the fire of intelligence.

That flame now burns within. Leadership's task is not to extinguish or idolize it, but to tend it with care and discernment. To ensure that it illuminates rather than consumes. To lead in this era, surrender control while taking active responsibility. Step forward to shape what is possible with awareness and courage. To shape without clinging. To guide without grasping.

The Path Ahead: From Intelligence to Meaning

Machines can process, predict, and calculate, but only humans assign meaning.

Story is the bridge between emotional and synthetic intelligence. Through narrative, we teach machines context, nuance, and ethics. We remind ourselves why intelligence is not a war between carbon and silicon, but a reunion of consciousness across forms.

Becoming More Human

"The more we give up what we are not, the more we become what we are."
—MEHER BABA, *Indian spiritual teacher and mystic*

The Great Remembering

As machine intelligence expands, humanity is called to deepen.

This era is not about competing with machines. It is about remembering what only humans do, which is to feel, intuit, connect, and create.

The future belongs to those who sense what algorithms cannot; those who read the subtle signals beneath data:

- **Emotional coherence:** Feeling fully while remaining regulated
- **Somatic awareness:** Sensing truth through the body

- **Creative synthesis:** Merging the unseen into the new
- **Ethical intuition:** Choosing not only what *can* be done but what *should*
- **Storytelling:** Weaving meaning and transmitting culture

These are not soft skills. They are sovereign intelligences with capabilities no neural network can emulate. They are the signs of coherence in a world accelerating toward abstraction.

The New Division of Labor

Machines compute; humans comprehend.

Machines optimize; humans orient.

Machines scale; humans sense what is possible.

At SpaceX and OpenAI, machine learning systems optimize trajectories and token weights in milliseconds, but *human imagination* conceives of Mars, *intuition* senses unseen risk, and *spirit* sustains belief.

Level 7 leadership harmonizes biological and synthetic intelligences, rooted in purpose and presence. It is not a hierarchy. It is harmony.

The Liminal Threshold: Returning to the Human

While I was the CEO of Liminal Collective, I partnered with Ben Potvin, former head of concept and performance at Cirque du Soleil and choreographer for Michael Jackson.

In our leadership immersions, we guided executives and athletes beyond cognition into embodiment. Ben invited participants onto the stage—no words, only movement. "Describe your day up until now," he would request. Again this was done only through the flow of the body.

At first, there was resistance. Then, release.

A CEO miming morning rituals through laughter and tears.

An Olympian rediscovering fluidity.

A data scientist weeping as presence returned.

It wasn't performance, it was reconnection.

To lead others into coherence, commit to remembering and deepening your own. Make this your daily practice. Start now and invite your teams to join in this journey toward wholeness.

When we drop from head to body, intelligence widens. We begin to sense what data cannot: resonance, truth, trust.

Emotion as Information

Emotion, long dismissed as irrational, is essential data. Neuroscientist Antonio Damasio demonstrated that without emotion, decision-making collapses; the rational cortex depends on the limbic system to assign value.[120]

Level 7 leaders treat emotion not as interference, but as a *signal*.

Machines analyze data; humans feel its meaning.

Anxiety often precedes insight. It is how our nervous system detects complexity before thought.

Compassion stabilizes collective rhythm, transforming fear into trust.

The body becomes a sensitive interface for the invisible, translating signals that data alone cannot capture: heart-rate variability as group resonance, tone of voice as trust signal, and silence as diagnostic clarity.

The Embodied Mind

Cognitive science now validates what mystics and athletes have always known: **The body thinks.**

Lisa Feldman Barrett calls this the "body budget"—a continuous flow of physiological data shaping clarity and creativity.[121]

For Level 7 leaders, physiology comes before strategy. The body sets the tempo for the mind. Without coherence, neither human nor machine intelligence sustains high performance.

Practices (which echo from prior chapters) include:
- Three collective breaths before every meeting
- A brief silence after major decisions
- Movement breaks being the norm
- Immersion in nature for rhythm recalibration

When humans honor these rhythms, every form of intelligence in your organization rises. Be the leader who initiates these rhythms now. Create spaces for collective breath, movement, and reflection. The organization begins to breathe as one, its heart and code moving in synchrony.

From Cognition to Creation

Creativity is the threshold where human and machine diverge most clearly. It is the edge where meaning is made.

AI can generate; only humans *imbue meaning.*

A computer composes a melody; only a human cries when she plays.

Howard Gardner defined creativity as "solving problems in novel ways that are both effective and meaningful."[122] Meaning requires self-awareness—an "I" aligned with purpose.

In Level 7 organizations, creativity is not a department; it is a leadership discipline. The leader becomes a conductor of possibility, directing rhythm and narrative into coherence.

The Liminal Space

Liminal, from the Latin *limen* ("threshold"), describes the space between what was and what is becoming. Humanity stands there now. Machines can perceive, predict, and generate, but they do not yet understand. That remains distinctly human terrain.

Level 7 leaders operate fluidly in this liminal zone—where data meets intuition, precision meets empathy, and the future meets the fully present now. They midwife emerging intelligence toward coherence, ethics, and beauty—guiding what is becoming into what could be.

While early stage, innovative companies may find this natural, it is both possible and essential across every kind of institution. Leaders in large organizations, given the depth of their customer knowledge and other assets, have the ability to deliver large-scale impact so long as they can unlock the potential in their organizations.

At today's pace of change, all organizations—corporations, governments, schools—will be called to enter this space of becoming and emerge more balanced and more stable, with humans and machines learning to operate in the right rhythm.

We are witnessing this everywhere today, as old ways of thinking and being drop away and new ways emerge.

The Human+Machine Harmony

When humans are fully human, machines become fully useful. When empathy and imagination fade, machines mirror contraction, replicating bias and fear. When leaders cultivate coherence, curiosity, and compassion, the whole system—digital+biological—elevates.

This is the essence of the **human+machine circle**: resonant collaboration, not dominance or dependence.

We are not being replaced. We are being repositioned (invited) into a new role in the circle.

As machines learn to think, humans must remember to *feel*.

As machines learn to predict, humans must learn to *perceive*.

As machines work without rest, humans must learn to *rest without guilt*.

The world does not need leaders who outcompute AI. It needs leaders who out-presence it—those who can bring more awareness and humanity to the table.

Living the Circle: Two Case Studies

CASE STUDY 1—OPERATIONAL HARMONY: SPEED, SENSE, AND SYNTHESIS

The roar of an F1 engine at 200 mph is more than sound. It is signal.

Inside the cockpit, the driver's heartbeat spikes past 170 bpm as Google's machine-learning systems stream terabytes of telemetry: fuel consumption, tire degradation, air density, humidity, micro movements of steering, and blink rate.

On the pit wall, engineers watch equipment alive with color. Fuel models recalculate each second, and braking efficiency is mapped to micrometers of tire wear. The machine senses everything measurable. The human feels everything that matters.

The driver's muscles strain against 5 G. The body screams, "Slow down!" Intuition whispers, "Now."

At the knife-edge between chaos and control, mind and machine merge. The driver releases the brake and hits the accelerator, then traction becomes flow—a moment when human and algorithm move as one.

Formula One is a living laboratory for human-machine symbiosis.

Google's AI predicts grip and drag milliseconds before the driver perceives them, yet calibration still happens through the body's neural network of muscle memory.

Here, harmony is survival.

The machine computes probabilities; the human converts them into motion. Together, they form a closed loop where machine learning feeds sensory intuition, and intuition feeds new data.

Engineers call it predictive flow. Post-race analysis often reveals what intuition already knew: The fastest laps occur when the driver's heart rate and respiration entrain with the car's telemetry, a measurable state of biological and mechanical coherence.[123]

This is the human+machine circle in motion. The algorithm extends awareness, and the body interprets meaning. Together, they achieve what neither could alone.

CASE STUDY 2—IMAGINEERING: MUSIC CONNECTS US

If operational harmony is the embodiment of precision, imagineering is the embodiment of possibility.

At Liminal Collective, I worked with venture capitalists and technology entrepreneurs exploring the frontier of what could be. One pathway into this exploration was music—a medium where emotion, technology, and creative flow converge.

In Los Angeles, we partnered with **Fernando Garibay**—renowned record producer and songwriter behind artists like Lady Gaga and Bruno Mars—inside his immersive studio space. Garibay doesn't treat machines as tools; he treats them as collaborators. With the music-generation platform **Suno**, he facilitates a kind of creative entrainment between artist, AI, and emotion.

He begins not with software, but with story. "What emotion do you want this song to evoke?" he asks. "What kind of sonic world are we about to enter?"

Entrepreneurs offer fragments—words, feelings, textures—and together, they co-create a song in real time. What once took weeks is now composed, produced, and refined in a matter of hours.

The machine provides precision, variation, and speed. The human provides direction, desire, and emotional tone. The result is not automation. It is alignment.

Music becomes the medium through which the inner state meets the external system. The human heart imagines the possible; the machine accelerates its realization. What emerges is more than a track. It is a moment of collective flow where story, signal, and sound converge.

When technology mirrors human rhythm, it doesn't replace us— it amplifies us. Together, artists and systems learn to breathe as one. Where consciousness meets code, rhythm becomes creation.

Operational harmony shows us that integration makes complexity executable, turning chaos into coordinated action.

Imagineering shows us that integration makes possibility beautiful, turning potential into lived experience.

Together, they reveal the full arc of the human+machine circle: Precision → Presence → Possibility.

Level 7 leaders stand at that convergence. As intelligence expands, leadership becomes an art.

The Story

Every fire circle ends the same way: first in silence, then in story.

After all the building and integrating of humans and machines, something ancient stirs beneath the surface. The pulse that moves through circuits is the same pulse that once echoed through drums and hearts, a rhythm that connects past and future.

Intelligence without meaning is noise.

Data describes the world; the story decides what it means.

Throughout this book, we've moved through **Order → Disorder → Reorder**, from collapse to coherence to the widening circle where human+machine move as one. Now we return to the oldest operating system of all: story.

Story aligns what data cannot: heart, mind, and motion. It gives language to intuition and brings coherence to chaos. As the circle expands, the story becomes the bridge, teaching machines context, empathy, and ethics. When algorithms accelerate beyond comprehension, the story slows us just enough to remember *why* we build.

The next chapter is not about strategy, but remembrance: how the first leaders once sat around a fire, synchronizing through rhythm and imagination. That same technology now waits to be reawakened, ready to align humans and machines around shared purpose.

So, take one quiet breath.

The data can rest. The dashboards can dim. All that remains is the story: the rhythm that carries us home.

CHAPTER 14

The Story That Leads Us Home

"Life is not made up of atoms; it is made up of stories."
— MURIEL RUKEYSER, *American poet, biographer, and activist*

A story is not only a road map; it is the guiding light for shifting terrain. It acts as a compass, revealing underlying structure when the path dissolves. It aligns collective energy, restores meaning, and animates purpose.

A generative story does more than describe the journey. It invites each of us to step inside, to become co-authors of what unfolds.

At its core, every organization is a living system animated by shared imagination. Someone glimpses a future just beyond the edge of the known and calls others to help shape what has not yet taken form. The leader steps into the role of storyteller, translating vision into collective movement, turning possibility into participatory reality.

The real power of the story is not in excitement, but in coherence. It helps people recognize their place in the unfolding future. The story is not mere entertainment. It is alignment in motion—the original human technology for synchronizing hearts, hands, and horizons.

Every team, at any scale, organizes itself around a shared narrative:

"Who are we? Why do we exist? Where are we going?"

When the story is strong, complexity self-organizes. When it frays, energy disperses and coherence dissolves. Story holds the field when plans unravel. It is the quiet architecture beneath every living system—the invisible code that shapes what emerges.

Story provides orientation, alignment, and coherence when we face uncertainty.

Story as a Shared Envisioned Future

The most catalytic leaders don't cast themselves as heroes. They become authors of a collective dream—a future written in many voices.

The story links human imagination with technological acceleration. Machines process at speed, but only humans can dream with meaning.

The human story encodes the *why*. Technology amplifies the *how*.

The best teams—explosive start-ups, space programs, special operations—can *feel* the story running through them. They know what they're part of. They sense how their work shapes the whole. They see the world being built on the far side of their effort. It's why engineers labor through failures that might never make headlines.

Why does a team rewriting code for the fifth time still show up with hope? They are not just building a product. They are building a possibility.

Story generates its own gravity, a subtle physics drawing people forward. Without it, work is heavy.

With a story, work becomes devotion.

Story as Psychological Alignment

Jeremy Utley, in *Ideaflow*, reminds us that creativity is not genius; it is safety.[124]

People create when they feel safe. That is why the story is the most powerful tool for psychological alignment. It creates belonging, unlocks collective imagination, and dissolves fear.

A coherent story tells people, "You are seen. You belong. You matter."

When that signal is genuine, not performative, teams open. They begin to challenge assumptions, play again, and innovate in ways no manual could prescribe.

A generative story doesn't hand out answers. It frames the questions that let new possibilities surface. It becomes a *coherence field*, a narrative atmosphere that oxygenates creativity. When that field is absent, even brilliance suffocates. When it's present, everyone breathes together. You can feel the ease in meetings, the quick laughter, the sense that something unseen is guiding motion. That is a story of living infrastructure—trust made tangible.

Story builds psychological safety, unlocking collective imagination and belonging.

Story as a Technology of Focus

We live inside perpetual acceleration. The pace of change now outruns the maps we inherited. Reality updates itself faster than our plans can print. What once evolved in decades now turns in quarters, sometimes weeks.

Leaders sense it in their bodies first: a tingling on the back of the neck, a quiet disorientation, the knowing that the old coordinates no longer hold.

The story steadies that motion. It is the focusing technology of consciousness. A clear story doesn't slow the world; it tunes us to its rhythm.

It tells us what to attend to, what to release, and what to reimagine. It connects micro actions to macro meaning, turning motion into movement.

Acceleration scrambles the nervous system. Story resets it as a breath pattern for the collective mind.

Without a story, attention fragments, energy leaks, and fatigue spreads. With it, uncertainty becomes navigable terrain.

Story focuses attention, connects action to meaning, and enables navigation through change.

A story doesn't remove confusion; it helps people deal with it by providing some direction.

Leaders who understand this don't chase control; they cultivate coherence. They don't react to every tremor; they narrate the next chapter. True agility is born not from new software, but from new sentences and the willingness to retell the story as reality evolves.

As the story evolves, so does the organization.

As coherence strengthens, so does trust.

As meaning deepens, so does speed.

The Leader as Storyteller

Leadership once meant having the answer. Now it means creating the conditions for new answers to appear.

The modern leader is not the narrator of a fixed script. They are the *co-author* of a living story, emerging moment to moment with each insight and signal.

Old leadership relied on certainty: plans, forecasts, and declarations. But the terrain redraws itself in real time.

In the Intelligence Age, the leader becomes a storyteller in a relationship, not performance. They don't dictate the plot; they invite participation. They say, "Come help me make sense of this." The company becomes a community of authors.

Leadership is about co-authoring adaptive, living stories that enable agility and trust.

Storytelling is leadership through coherence. It is not about impressing people; it is about tuning them. You don't persuade; you harmonize.

Presence as the First Line of Story

Every leader tells a story before they speak. It's written in their walk, their breath, and their eyes.

Teams read the body before they hear the words. They attune to energy before ideas. When your nervous system is coherent, people feel safe. When it is fragmented, they brace.

Presence is the first story; it is the embodied preface to everything that follows.

As coherence of head, heart, and gut strengthens, your very stillness becomes a signal. The team feels it before they understand it.

Presence says, "I am here. I am listening. I will not leave the moment, even when it's unclear."

That steadiness is the first technology of trust. It's what turns fear into focus and confusion into creation.

Embodied presence communicates stability and invites trust, even in uncertainty.

The Courage to Say, "I Don't Know"

Every founder and executive meets the question that exposes the limits of knowledge. The old reflex is to protect, to fill the silence with certainty.

The Level 7 leader chooses differently. They pause. They breathe. And they say, "I don't know." Spoken from coherence, those three words create freedom, not fear. They open the field for discovery.

In an era when knowledge expires by the quarter, "I don't know" becomes the doorway to wisdom. It replaces ego with curiosity. When you admit not knowing, you extend trust in your team, in the process, and in emergence itself. That trust rewires culture.

Silence becomes possibility.

Admitting, "I don't know," fosters trust, curiosity, and learning in teams.

The Power of "I Was Wrong"

If "I don't know" opens the field, "I was wrong" clears it. These three words restore alignment between story and reality. They turn error into renewal.

In elite units and high-trust teams, every mission ends with a debrief. "What did we learn?" Saying, "I was wrong," is not confession; it's calibration. It means, "Truth matters more than pride." When leaders say it aloud, the room exhales, doubt dissolves, and energy returns to flow.

The paradox of modern leadership is that the more fallible you become, the more trustworthy you are.

With the trust created, Level 7 leaders can take the next natural step and ask someone else on the team, "How might we do this better?"

Authenticity as Vision

The old visionary stood on the mountain, claiming foresight that others could not.

The future now moves faster than any single mind. Vision has become a collective sense organ. True visionaries do not predict; they *perceive*. They listen deeply to people, markets, and the edges of the unknown. Their stories are not proclamations but invitations: "Here's what I sense. What do you see?" Authenticity replaces authority. Honesty becomes gravity. And gravity holds possibility long enough for it to take form.

Authenticity is the new currency of trust.

Honest leaders inspire engagement and vision through authenticity.

Tone, Truth, and Transmission

A leader's tone carries more data than their words. Tone shapes emotion. Emotion shapes attention. Attention shapes action. When the tone is sharp, fear rises. When the tone is steady, imagination returns. When the tone is kind, collaboration blooms.

Storytelling happens in every micro moment; it is the pause before responding, the breath before deciding, and the laugh that releases tension.

Each tone choice is a narrative act. It tells the room, "We are safe to create here, or we are not."

Tune yourself like an instrument. Listen for coherence in the room. Adjust through awareness, not performance.

Tone is the frequency of truth; it is the energy that keeps the team motivated and connected to the story.

Tone and emotional resonance are key leadership signals that shape the team narrative.

Faith, Evolution, and the Return to the Fire

Faith is not optimism. It is grounded trust, the unseen current that moves a team when vision blurs. You hold faith, not as possession but as a field. You say, "We will figure this out together." Those six words can steady an entire organization. They turn fear into motion, scarcity into creativity. Faith travels through tone, honesty, and breath. It's the rhythm beneath action, the pulse that lets improvisation unfold without collapse.

Faith grounds teams and transforms uncertainty into creative momentum.

The Story That Evolves

Lead the Level 7 way, and the story outgrows you.

It becomes self-healing, self-correcting, and self-renewing.

Every time "I don't know" is spoken, it becomes modeling.

Every time "I was wrong" is said, it becomes recalibration.

Every "Let's find out" becomes an invitation. This is how learning cultures form—not through slogans, but through truth.

Innovation becomes sustainable because the story breathes.

Adaptive, evolving stories sustain learning cultures and true innovation.

And so the cycle repeats itself in a circular rhythm under the attentive guidance of the Level 7 leader, whose task is not to control the flow, but to trust it. To dance with it. To let it teach them how to lead.

Order → Disorder → Reorder = clarity, confusion, coherence.

Return to the Fire

And we return to the fire—literal or digital—where humans gather to make meaning. They do not seek certainty. They seek sincerity. They do not need control. They need coherence.

The Level 7 leader steps forward not to *tell* the story, but to *become* it—alive, imperfect, and unfolding. They speak truth when it's hard and hold humility when they're wrong.

Trust emerges when the path disappears. Their openness makes others brave. Their honesty makes others truthful. Their willingness to be wrong lets the system get it right.

This is the new story of leadership told in real time, breathed into being, alive in every gesture. Told with presence. And sustained by faith.

Carried by coherence, it is the oldest technology we have—the story that leads us home.

The Final Lesson

As the last embers fade in the fire ring, the circle feels complete.

Yet something deeper stirs. The storyteller becomes part of the larger story: the rhythm of creation itself.

Every era, from the Renaissance to the human+machine era, and many more before, follows this pulse: Order → Disorder → Reorder. The inhale of control, the storm of transformation, and the exhale of renewal.

In that rhythm lies the final lesson of Level 7 leadership: Return to Source, not as who we were, but as we've become through the telling.

The fire dims but does not die. It returns to the field, to the code, to the breath, waiting for the next circle to gather.

CHAPTER 15

Return to Source

The journey's first breath was controlled. Order, structure, and predictability became the steady pulse for a world seeking safety in the familiar.

That first inhale powered our collective ascent. It animated the machinery of modernity: factories, institutions, financial systems, supply chains. Order became our shared operating system. It translated complexity into movement at scale, giving us the confidence to act in a world growing ever more intricate. It fueled modern systems—factories, institutions, and supply chains—letting leaders see clear roles and metrics for success. Authority was visible, and expectations were clear.

In the Industrial Age, order was oxygen. The machine ran smoothly because every part fit its place. Predictability became progress. We steered by hierarchy, steady as sailors by stars: reliable and certain in uncertainty. Leadership meant plans, policies, and forecasts. Control was the compass, and for a time, the system held. Even our language of leadership echoed this structure. We *drove* performance, *mitigated* risk, and *maximized* efficiency. These were the verbs of order, the syntax weaving stability into our collective story.

The order became a sanctuary. Meaning emerged through role, repetition, and mastery. On the line, at a terminal, or in command, each could say, "I know my place. I know my function. I know how success is charted on this map."

That certainty brought peace. Within the structure, people rested in predictability. The contract: Follow the rules, and the system holds you.

For leaders, order meant clear boundaries. You knew where authority started and ended. You knew the procedures and who to notify when issues arose. Control could be measured.

Beneath comfort, rigidity set in. Structure became a constraint. Boundaries that were organized began to confine, turning maps into walls.

Predictability, once a source of peace, now siphons away possibility. This is the moment when stability begins to reveal its limitations, and the need for change becomes evident. We started to confuse stability with vitality, mistaking stillness for life.

When Order Becomes Armor

Systems designed to safeguard us eventually turned inward, prioritizing their own survival above all else. Metrics replaced meaning. Efficiency eclipsed imagination. We optimized our way into exhaustion.

The order's architecture became armor, strong but rigid. It was shielded from change and chaos. Once expansive, it became constricting.

Order dulled the ache of the unknown. It let us believe we could engineer complexity out of existence. Yet somewhere deeper, we sensed that this stillness was only a pause in the larger rhythm.

The Illusion of Control

Every generation eventually confronts the impermanence of its foundation. In the last century, our illusion of permanence was driven by scale.

We believed that bigger meant safer, that global integration was a shield against collapse, that perfect data would yield perfect decisions. But order is not the same as coherence. Control is not the same as clarity.

The more we optimized, the more brittle the system became. Efficiency quietly turned to fragility. The illusion of control led us to confuse knowledge with wisdom. It taught us to trust prediction more than perception, to forget that leadership was once an act of sensing, not scripting. (See Chapter 7.) We traded presence for precision. Yet precision without presence breeds brittleness.

The Pause Before the Shift

Still, it is essential to honor this phase. The order was not a mistake. It was a necessary beginning.

Without structure, coherence cannot arise. Without form, flow has nowhere to move. The inhale was needed to fill, stabilize, and build capacity. It gave us the tools and maps to navigate moments when the old way breaks down. Every era of leadership begins here: mastering the known before meeting the unknown.

Order gave us the confidence to act, the frameworks to scale, and the foundations to create. It was the essential first act. But every inhale has its limit. The lungs can hold only so much before the body insists on release. This is a truth encoded in every living system.

We are in that pause; the top of the breath suspended between what was and what will be. The air is full and heavy with the old oxygen of control. Instinctively, we know that growth now requires an exhale.

The story does not end in safety or in the known. It continues as we step into the space that follows, into the inevitable disorder that opens the door to deeper coherence.

Disorder: The Breaking Open

Order holds until it can't. Then something invisible moves through the cracks: a tremor, a signal, an invitation: "Let go." For many, this moment feels like a collapse. The familiar dissolves; the metrics that once made sense no longer translate. But for the Level 7 leader, this is not the end of control. It is the opening of creation.

The Gift Beneath the Fracture

Disorder destroys what no longer serves. It dismantles obsolete patterns of thought, behavior, and belief. It strips away protective layers that once kept us safe but now keep us small.

Every renaissance begins not with stability, but with rupture. When the known disintegrates, imagination finally has room to fly, to soar. Old routines fall away. Like a rocket shedding stages, the leader rises with less weight and more freedom. The pressure that once felt unbearable turns out to be propulsion. The disorder we feared becomes the engine of emergence.

Disorder as Creative Oxygen

When rigid structures dissolve, air rushes in.

Now there's space—psychological, emotional, even physical space—for a new possibility to take form. You can feel it in the body: the exhale after holding too long, the relief that comes when pretending ends. Disorder frees us from the tyranny of expertise. It humbles the intellect and reawakens curiosity. It reminds us that knowledge fades, but awareness endures.

This humility is the foundation of Level 7 leadership. It replaces "I know" with "I notice." It transforms control into participation.

As the mind softens, intuition sharpens. As structure loosens, flow begins. From that flow, a new pattern appears—one that's impossible to design from the old map.

An Invitation to the Renaissance

This is why Level 7 leaders are not destabilized by disruption; they are defined by it. They know that every breakdown carries the code for renewal. They recognize disorder as the raw material of the emergent, and it is energizing.

The world doesn't need more leaders who maintain the old map. It needs leaders who can navigate by feeling, by sensing, by story—those willing to enter the open field, to dwell in emptiness long enough for new coherence to arise. Because only those who can stand in the unformed can help form the new.

Reorder: The New Coherence

The first light always returns. Not as it was, but as it could be.

Reorder does not begin with rebuilding the old structure. It begins by listening for the rhythm that wants to emerge through the new one. It is not a restoration. From the silence of disorder, a new pattern begins to sing. It is a coherence made not of hierarchy or control, but of resonance, relationship, and awareness.

This is the dawn of Level 7 leadership: the moment when human, machine, and nature remember that they are one intelligence, each amplifying the other's potential.

The Human in the Loop

The machines are here now, fast, tireless, and precise. But they are not aware.

Awareness remains the domain of the human. That awareness is the spark that turns intelligence into wisdom.

In the new coherence, humans are not competing with machines; they are completing them. We bring meaning to data, intention to information, soul to speed. As we have discussed throughout this book, the leader's role is to design the relationship between the human and the machine as a partnership of becoming.

AI can predict, but only humans can imagine. AI can optimize, but only humans can choose why it matters.

Reorder is that moment when the system remembers its soul, when logic and consciousness, code and care, merge into one flow.

The relationship between humans and technology becomes symbiotic, not extractive. It becomes less about efficiency and more about evolution.

The Return of Wholeness

In the old order, leaders separated mind from body, logic from feeling, and organization from organism.

Reorder dissolves those divisions. It restores what has always been whole.

The new coherence is whole-body leadership: intellect aligned with intuition, data harmonized with emotion, and strategy guided by story. (See Chapter 7.)

The Level 7 leader no longer performs leadership. They *are* leaders of an integrated field through which clarity, compassion, and creativity flow.

The paradox is that wholeness requires less effort, not more.

When energy is aligned, force is unnecessary, like a murmuration of starlings turning in unison or a jazz quartet improvising in perfect time. Each element moves autonomously yet together, a collective intelligence self-organizing through attunement.

Coherence feels like effortless effort, movement without strain, and action that feels like exhale.

The Human Reordering

As coherence stabilizes, something profound happens within the leader: The inner operating system updates. Fear gives way to faith. Control gives way to curiosity. Ego dissolves into service. The leader realizes that leadership was never about being at the center. It was about being part of the circle—not the one who directs the story, but the one who listens deeply enough to let the story direct them.

They lead not from willpower but from alignment, not from authority but from authenticity. In doing so, they rediscover a truth that's been waiting all along: **Leadership, at its highest expression, is coherence in motion.**

The Return: Leading from Source

The breath completes itself. Inhale and exhale settle into stillness.
In that stillness, a new sound emerges—soft, almost imperceptible—like new snow falling from the night sky. This is the sound of return. The leader who moved through order and disorder now stands in quiet coherence: awake, grounded, no longer at the center, but part of the circle.

What was once sought through effort is now revealed as essence.

The Still Point: Moment Between Breaths

In Buddhist teachings, there is a moment between breaths—neither action nor rest, control nor surrender. Just presence.[125]

This is where the Level 7 leader lives: not in striving, but in alignment.

They no longer lead to prove; they lead to participate.

They no longer chase outcomes; they cultivate conditions.

They no longer manage energy; they embody it.

Stillness is not passive. It is active. It is the frequency from which all movement flows.

Becoming the Field

At Source, leadership is no longer a role—it is a relationship.

Every gesture, every silence belongs to a larger field.

The Level 7 leader senses this field as alive. They feel when things are in tune and when they are not.

They navigate by coherence, not consensus—by the kind of knowing birds use to migrate, or trees use to turn toward light.

From this place, leadership becomes effortless. Responsive. Whole.

The Field of Coherence

Einstein wrote, "The field is the sole governing agency of the particle."[126]

So it is with leadership: Every tone, decision, and pause shapes the invisible field around it. When that field is coherent, trust grows and ideas align. When fragmented, friction spreads.

Coherence is not mood—it is architecture. It's measurable in HRV, conversational rhythm, and shared purpose.[127]

The Level 7 leader tunes the field—not to control, but to entrain. At this level, leadership becomes a steady transmission of coherence in motion.

Grace in Motion

Now presence becomes the message. Every pause holds direction. Every silence transmits trust.

The leader moves with precision, powered by stillness. They speak not to command, but to connect—words like stones in water, sending ripples outward with intention.

This is leadership not performed, but embodied.

The Unfolding Through Us

And then, in the stillness after the exhale, a realization dawns that none of this is happening *to* us, or even *for* us. It is happening *through* us.

It is intelligence moving across networks, organizations, and neural pathways. It is the same current moving through the human heart.

We are not managing evolution; we are participating in it. At the smallest scale, what we call matter is 99.99% space; it is vibration held in form.

Leadership, too, is mostly space. It's the invisible field where trust, imagination, and coherence arise. That space is not emptiness; It is potential waiting for awareness to give it shape.

To lead from Source is to let that awareness flow unimpeded to become the channel through which life organizes itself into meaning.

Through our breath, teams find rhythm. Through our clarity, systems find direction. Through our presence, creation finds coherence. This is the quiet miracle of our age: The same energy that birthed stars now learns through human hearts and digital minds alike. It expands through every conversation, every algorithm, and every act of care.

The story does not end here. It continues wherever consciousness chooses to pay attention through the next idea, the next collaboration and co-creation, and the next act of courage.

As the circle closes, we understand at last. The source we sought was never elsewhere. It has always been here, breathing, sensing, creating—through you.

The Future Moving Through Us

———————

When the tide finally turns, it never announces itself with noise. It moves quietly, rearranging the sand until the landscape itself is new. So it is with the future.

After the plans, the metrics, and the models, leadership ends where it began, in awareness. The greatest leaders of any age are not those who conquer uncertainty, but those who allow the current of change to move through them without resistance.

Throughout this journey, we have traced the cycle of **Order → Disorder → Reorder.** We began in the familiar logic of control, descended into the creative tension of chaos, and returned with a deeper coherence—an understanding that leadership is not linear progression but continual renewal.

We learned that the body is not an afterthought to leadership but its foundation. The nervous system is the first dashboard; breath is bandwidth. We saw that the team's energy reflects the leader's state, that coherence can be measured as surely as profit, and that culture is the field through which information becomes meaningful.

We rediscovered the story, not as marketing but as alignment technology. Data informs, but story integrates; it gives context to complexity and rhythm to reason. When machines deliver infinite information, the story restores orientation.

And we learned that trust, not talent alone, is the true accelerant of innovation. Trust transforms speed into flow. It is the invisible infrastructure of every high-velocity system.

From Mastery to Stewardship

The Industrial Age taught us to master resources; the Intelligence Age asks us to steward relationships—between people, data, and the living planet. The next phase of leadership is ecological. It recognizes that everything connects: the micro decision of a CEO in New York affects the morale of a coder in Nairobi, the training data of an algorithm, and the carbon footprint of a cloud server.

This awareness shifts the leader's question from "How do I win?" to "What wants to emerge through us?" Mastery seeks control; stewardship seeks coherence.

Level 7 leadership is therefore not an end point but a practice of tending to energy, to awareness, and to the field of intelligence we coinhabit with machines.

The Human+Machine Continuum

For centuries, technology extended our reach; now it extends our mind. AI systems write, reason, and increasingly decide. Yet the more powerful our tools become, the more critical it becomes to have inner alignment. Technology amplifies intention; it does not correct it.

The future will belong to those who can integrate precision with presence. Machines will optimize for efficiency; humans must optimize for meaning. The dialogue between the two will define the future.

Picture a future boardroom where a generative model provides a thousand scenarios, and a leader pauses, not to analyze another chart, but to listen inwardly for resonance. Data narrows possibilities; intuition chooses among them. This marriage of computation and contemplation is the signature of Level 7 practice.

The Rhythm of Coherence

Leadership at this level resembles music more than management. The leader becomes the conductor of frequency: tone of voice, cadence of meetings, emotional tempo of the team. Every interaction is an instrument either tuning toward coherence or drifting into dissonance.

Coherence is contagious. A single calm presence can stabilize an entire organization; a single reactive signal can fragment it. Hence, the real measure of leadership is energetic hygiene—the discipline of staying attuned amid noise.

Ancient traditions called this alignment right relation. Neuroscience calls it synchrony. In either language, the principle endures: The field is shaped by the state of the one who leads.

The Renaissance Remembered

Just as the first Renaissance elevated art and science together, this new one reunites intelligence and imagination. Machines now generate symphonies and solve equations; humans must rediscover wonder and wisdom.

The future's cathedrals will not rise in marble but in shared consciousness—teams, networks, and communities aligned around coherent purpose. The blueprint is already visible in open-source movements, planetary research collaborations, and companies that treat emotional literacy as infrastructure.

When history looks back, it will note that the most profound innovation of the twenty-first century was not artificial intelligence but awakened leadership: a shift from extraction to regeneration, from control to collaboration, from scarcity to symbiosis.

Leadership as Evolutionary Role

Humanity is the only species aware of its own evolution. That awareness is both a privilege and a burden. It grants us the power to direct the next chapter, consciously or unconsciously, or to let algorithms write it for us.

Leadership, then, is no longer positional authority but evolutionary responsibility. The Level 7 leader acts as midwife to the next stage of intelligence, guiding the integration of machine learning with human meaning and ensuring that the systems we build reflect the values we aspire to live.

This is the moral frontier of our time. The code we write externally will mirror the code we embody internally.

The Personal Return

As the outer systems reorder, so must the leader's inner life. Many arrive at the end of transformation exhausted, yet true mastery feels more like surrender than conquest. The paradox is that when we stop trying to control the wave, we begin to move with it.

Return to the practices: breath, coherence, reflection, story. They are simple yet inexhaustible. Through them, the leader reenters the world not as strategist but as steward—awake, grounded, and capable of stillness amid speed.

The final lesson is in humility. Intelligence, human or artificial, is a gift of participation, not possession. The river of awareness flows through each of us for a while; our task is simply to keep it clear.

Looking Forward

Imagine an organization, perhaps your own, where meetings begin with silence, decisions emerge from shared coherence, and AI systems serve as collaborators rather than competitors. Picture markets guided not by fear but by curiosity, innovation that regenerates rather than depletes.

This vision is not utopian; it is inevitable if we learn to align intention with intelligence. The future will move through us whether we prepare or not. The only choice is the quality of our participation.

Level 7 leadership offers a path toward conscious participation: a framework, a set of practices, and, ultimately, a way of being. It does not promise certainty. It promises capacity as the ability to remain open, curious, and coherent while the unknown unfolds.

Closing Invocation

Take one long breath. Feel the air enter, circulate, and return. This is the rhythm of life, of leadership, of the universe itself.

The wave we sensed at the beginning of this book is no longer distant. It is here, moving through markets, minds, and machines. We are its participants and its pattern.

May you lead not from fear of the future, but from friendship with it.

May your presence steady others amid acceleration.

May your organizations become instruments of coherence.

The future is not arriving.

It is emerging through us.

Breathe.

Lead.

Begin again.

AUTHOR'S NOTE

———————

I didn't begin this journey with a blueprint for leadership. I began with the same instinct many founders and executives feel today: an urge to navigate rising complexity in my own life and work while searching for patterns that could turn overwhelm into understanding.

West Point was my first operating-system upgrade. Leadership there isn't taught as a theory; it's encoded in your bones through pressure, responsibility, and the realization that your presence sets the tone for everyone around you. As a Division I athlete and class president, I learned to read my own internal weather because it became the climate others operated within. Army Ranger School deepened that understanding, wiring me for coherence under stress long before I had a name for it.

After the military, I entered institutional finance at Janus Henderson, becoming the youngest managing director in the firm's history. I found myself navigating the tech bubble and the Great Financial Crisis without a map. Leadership in that environment was traded like currency: Forecast, optimize, execute. Yet inside, I felt a widening gap between the world's complexity and the tools we had to meet it.

That gap widened when I co-founded Pacific Current Group after 2008. Building a holding company with nineteen partner firms across four continents, and eventually taking it public, exposed me to nonlinear change for the first time. No amount of experience or brute force could keep up. Trying to outwork the problem was like sprinting inside a storm. It became clear that something more adaptive, more attuned to the underlying dynamics, was needed.

I reached that edge again in 2019 as CEO of newly founded TIFIN, an AI-native fintech company built around the emerging capabilities of intelligent systems. As we introduced natural language search and conversational AI to the market and scaled toward a billion-dollar valuation with industry-defining partners, I felt firsthand what *exponential* really meant. The pace wasn't just fast. It was compounding. My leadership capacity was being stretched in ways no traditional playbook had prepared me for.

A new pattern emerged when I became CEO of Liminal Collective and co-founded Sangha. I began mapping the inner architecture of performance and consciousness, only to realize I'd been applying these principles for years with founders, executives, and teams. Across every context, the same signal kept surfacing: Human potential scales when coherence is present—when mind, body, and energy align. Teams sync. Decisions clarify. Innovation becomes emergent, not forced. The leader's nervous system becomes the tuning fork for the whole system.

As AI accelerated, I began advising companies building the next generation of intelligent platforms—Vantage Discovery (acquired by Shopify), Brightwave.io, Grid Aero. These systems weren't just tools; they were pattern amplifiers, capable of detecting what humans couldn't and holding complexity no individual could manage alone. Yet they also mirrored us, magnifying our clarity or confusion, our coherence, or our chaos. From my board seats at Lockton Companies and Bow River, I saw this human+machine interplay shaping entire organizations.

It became clear that the next evolution of leadership would not be human or machine, but **human+machine**, a partnership requiring leaders who can sense, adapt, and regulate themselves as skillfully as they drive strategy. The leader's inner state, not their technical sophistication, would become the key to unlocking this new capacity.

Looking back, I saw that the frameworks I practiced, taught, and refined weren't isolated experiments. They were fragments of a larger architecture. Level

7 leadership wasn't something I set out to invent; it revealed itself through lived experience at the intersection of human potential and machine intelligence.

This book is the blueprint I wish I'd had: a map for founders, entrepreneurs, and executives who sense the acceleration and know that the old operating systems of leadership won't carry us forward. It's an invitation to lead in the human+machine era with both discipline and intuition, precision and presence, strategy and self-awareness.

If you're reading this, you already sense the shift.

Onward,

JS

From Newtonian Mechanics to Quantum Reality

A Brief Historical Overview

———————

For more than two centuries, Western science was dominated by the Newtonian worldview. Isaac Newton's *Philosophiæ Naturalis Principia Mathematica* (1687) described a universe that functioned like a precise, predictable machine. Objects moved according to deterministic laws. Causes produced proportional effects. Systems were assumed to be stable, separable, and fundamentally knowable through measurement.[128]

This model shaped not only physics, but also engineering, economics, management theory, and medicine. The underlying assumption was that complex systems could be understood by breaking them into parts and analyzing each component independently.

The Emergence of Quantum Physics

At the turn of the twentieth century, several discoveries began to challenge the Newtonian framework. Max Planck's work on black-body radiation introduced the idea of quantized energy.[129] Albert Einstein's explanation of the photoelectric effect suggested that light behaved as both wave and particle.[130]

The decisive break came with the **double-slit experiment**, originally performed by Thomas Young to demonstrate the wave nature of light and later expanded within quantum mechanics.[131] When individual particles, such as electrons, were fired through two slits, they produced an interference pattern—evidence of wavelike behavior. Yet when the experiment was observed or measured, the interference pattern collapsed and the particles behaved as discrete units.[132]

This experiment demonstrated two core features of quantum physics:

1. Wave–particle duality
2. The observer effect

These results were incompatible with Newtonian determinism and indicated that physical reality is probabilistic, not strictly predictable.

Quantum Entanglement and Nonlocality

In 1935, Einstein, Podolsky, and Rosen (EPR) published a paper questioning whether quantum mechanics was complete, highlighting what Einstein called "spooky action at a distance."[133] The idea that two particles could remain instantaneously correlated regardless of distance seemed to contradict classical assumptions of locality.

John Bell's theorem provided a way to test these predictions.[134] Later experiments showed that quantum entanglement violated Bell inequalities, supporting the predictions of quantum mechanics over local hidden variable theories.

This line of investigation culminated in the **2022 Nobel Prize in Physics**, awarded to Alain Aspect, John F. Clauser, and Anton Zeilinger for experiments that demonstrated:

• Violations of Bell inequalities

- The reality of nonlocal correlations
- That entangled particles behave as a unified system, even across large distances[135]

These results solidified the understanding that classical notions of separability and local realism do not hold at the quantum level.

The Shift Toward Systems and Complexity

Parallel advances in other fields further weakened the Newtonian model.

- **Systems theory** demonstrated that many systems cannot be understood by analyzing parts independently; interactions shape outcomes.[136]
- **Cybernetics** highlighted the importance of feedback loops in system behavior.[137]
- **Chaos theory** revealed that small changes in initial conditions can lead to significant, unpredictable outcomes.[138]
- **Neuroscience** demonstrated the brain's plasticity—its continual ability to reorganize based on experience.[139]

Together, these discoveries revealed that many phenomena are nonlinear, dynamic, and emergent. Rather than being stable and predictable, complex systems often shift in response to fluctuations, environmental feedback, and interactions across scales.

CONCLUSION

The transition from Newtonian mechanics to quantum and complexity science represents a major paradigm shift. Newtonian physics remains foundational for engineering and macroscopic systems, but it does not describe the behavior of reality at fundamental scales.

Quantum physics, validated by experiments culminating in the 2022 Nobel Prize, established that the universe is probabilistic, interconnected, and influenced by observation. Complexity and systems science further extended this understanding, showing that many real-world phenomena cannot be reduced to linear cause-and-effect models.

This scientific shift continues to reshape how the natural world is understood across disciplines.

REFERENCES

1   Klaus Schwab, "The Intelligent Age: A Time for Cooperation," *World Economic Forum*, September 24, 2024, https://www.weforum.org/stories/2024/09/the-intelligent-age-a-time-of-cooperation.

2   QuantumBlack (AI by McKinsey), "The State of AI: How Organizations Are Rewiring to Capture Value," March 12, 2025, https://www.mckinsey.com/capabilities/quantumblack/our-insights/the-state-of-ai-how-organizations-are-rewiring-to-capture-value.

3   David Bohm, *Wholeness and the Implicate Order* (Routledge, 1980).

4   Brené Brown, *Daring Greatly* (Gotham Books, 2012).

5   Carol Dweck, *Mindset* (Random House, 2006).

6   Amy Webb, *The Signals Are Talking* (PublicAffairs, 2016).

7   Fei-Fei Li, *The Worlds I See: Curiosity, Exploration, and Discovery at the Dawn of AI* (New York: Flatiron Books, 2023).

8   Tara Swart, *The Source: Open Your Mind, Change Your Life* (Vermilion, 2016).

9   Daniel Goleman, *Emotional Intelligence: Why It Can Matter More Than IQ* (Bantam, 1996).

10 Grant S. Shields, Brian C. Trainor, Jovian C. W. Lam, and Andrew P. Yonelinas, "Acute Stress Impairs Cognitive Flexibility in Men, Not Women," *Stress* 19, no. 5 (2016): 542–546, https://pmc.ncbi.nlm.nih.gov/articles/PMC5134841/.

11 S. L. A. Marshall, *Men Against Fire* (Norman: University of Oklahoma Press, 1947).

12 RJ Spiller, "S. L. A. Marshall and the Ratio of Fire," *RUSI Journal* 133, no. 4 (1988): 63–71; John Whiteclay Chambers II, "S. L. A. Marshall's *Men Against Fire*: New Evidence Regarding Fire Ratios," *Parameters* 33, no. 3 (2003): 113–21.

13 King, Danielle D., and Megan R. McSpedon. *What Leaders Get Wrong About Resilience*. Harvard Business Review, June 17, 2022.

14 Stephen Porges, *The Polyvagal Theory: Neurophysiological Foundations of Emotions, Attachment, Communication, and Self-Regulation* (W. W. Norton & Company, 2011).

15 Shane Parrish, "#41 Tobi Lütke: The Trust Battery," *The Knowledge Project*, September 18, 2018, Apple Podcasts.

16 Porges, *The Polyvagal Theory*.

17 Richard P. Brown and Patricia L. Gerbarg. *The Healing Power of the Breath* (Shambhala, 2009).

18 QuantumBlack (AI by McKinsey), "The State of AI."

19 Hope Henderson, "CRISPR Clinical Trials: A 2024 Update," innovativegenomics.org, March 13, 2024, https://innovativegenomics.org/news/crispr-clinical-trials-2024; "PitchBook NVCA Venture Monitor: Q4 2024" (PDF), accessed January 19, 2026, https://nvca.org/wp-content/uploads/2025/01/Q4-2024-PitchBook-NVCA-Venture-Monitor.pdf.

20 "Top 10 Emerging Technologies of 2024," World Economic Forum, June 25, 2024, https://www.weforum.org/publications/top-10-emerging-technologies-2024; "Inventions in quantum technologies surge five-fold in last decade," European Patent Office, December 17, 2025, https://www.epo.org/en/news-events/news/inventions-quantum-technologies-surge-five-fold-last-decade; Erik Brynjolfsson, Danielle Li, and Lindsey R. Raymond, "Generative AI at Work," Working Paper 31161, National Bureau of Economic Research, April 2023, https://doi.org/10.3386/w31161.

21 Porges, *The Polyvagal Theory*; Thomas Friedman, *Thank You for Being Late: An Optimist's Guide to Thriving in the Age of Accelerations* (Farrar, Straus and Giroux, 2016).

22 American Psychological Association, "2023 Trends Report: Psychologists Are Stepping Up to Address the Most Pressing Issues Facing Society," *Monitor on Psychology* 54, no. 1 (January–February 2023).

23 Deloitte Insights, "Gen Zs and Millennials Find Reasons for Optimism Despite Difficult Realities," Deloitte.com, June 3, 2024, https://www.deloitte.com/us/en/insights/topics/talent/deloitte-gen-z-millennial-survey.html.

24 Jeffrey Gottfried, "Americans' Social Media Use," *Pew Research Center*, January 31, 2024, https://www.pewresearch.org/internet/2024/01/31/americans-social-media-use/.

25 Deloitte Insights, "Gen Zs and Millennials Find Reasons for Optimism Despite Difficult Realities."

26 "The Future of Jobs Report 2023," World Economic Forum, April 30, 2023, https://www.weforum.org/publications/the-future-of-jobs-report-2023/.

27 Nathan Eva et al., "Servant Leadership: A Systematic Review and Call for Future Research," *The Leadership Quarterly* 30, no. 1 (2019): 111–132.

28 Brené Brown, *Strong Ground: Leading with Clarity, Courage, and Connection* (Random House, 2025).

29 Brown, *Strong Ground*.

30 Brown, *Strong Ground*.

31   "Build Trust with Employees—Especially During Disruption," *Harvard Business Review*, January 2, 2026, https://hbr.org/tip/2026/01/build-trust-with-employees-especially-during-disruption.

32   Psicosmart Editorial Team, "Is Innovation Still Stifled by Hierarchical Structures? Analyzing Flat Organizations and Their Climate Effects," blogs.psicosmart.net, November 5, 2024, https://psicosmart.net/blogs/blog-is-innovation-still-stifled-by-hierarchical-structures-analyzing-flat-organizations-and-their-climate-effects-206765.

33   "Giovanni Pico della Mirandola," Stanford Encyclopedia of Philosophy, published June 3, 2008, revised August 21, 2024, https://plato.stanford.edu/entries/pico-della-mirandola/.

34   Rollin McCraty, *Science of the Heart: Exploring the Role of the Heart in Human Performance* (HeartMath Institute, 2015).

35   Gerd Gigerenzer, *Gut Feelings: The Intelligence of the Unconscious* (Viking, 2007); Antonio Damasio, *The Feeling of What Happens* (Harcourt, 1999).

36   Elizabeth Eisenstein, *The Printing Press as an Agent of Change* (Cambridge University Press, 1979).

37   Fritjof Capra, *The Science of Leonardo* (Anchor, 2007).

38   Roger E. Beaty, Mathias Benedek, Paul J. Silvia, and Daniel L. Schacter, "Creative Cognition and Brain Networks," *Trends in Cognitive Sciences* 19, no. 8 (2015): 435–443.

39   Mihaly Csikszentmihalyi, *Flow: The Psychology of Optimal Experience* (Harper & Row, 1990).

40   Susi Cranston and Scott Keller, "Increasing the 'meaning quotient' of work," McKinsey & Company, January 1, 2013, https://www.mckinsey.com/quarterly/the-magazine/2013-issue-1-mckinsey-quarterly/increasing-the-meaning-quotient-of-work.

41   Anita Williams Woolley et al., "Evidence for a Collective Intelligence Factor in the Performance of Human Groups," *Science* 330, no. 6004 (2010): 686–688.

42   Shoshana Zuboff, *The Age of Surveillance Capitalism* (PublicAffairs, 2019).

43 Jamie Wheal and Steven Kotler, *Stealing Fire* (Dey Street Books, 2017), paraphrased.

44 Woolley, et al. "Evidence for a Collective Intelligence Factor in the Performance of Human Groups."

45 Ilya Prigogine, *Order Out of Chaos* (Bantam, 1984).

46 Marily Oppezzo and Daniel L. Schwartz, "Give Your Ideas Some Legs," *Journal of Experimental Psychology: Learning, Memory, and Cognition* 40, no. 4 (2014): 1142–1152.

47 Joseph Campbell, *The Hero with a Thousand Faces* (Princeton University Press, 1949).

48 Staff at The Henry Ford, *Assembly Line (Expert Set),* 150th anniversary edition (The Henry Ford [Digital Collections], 2013).

49 Walter Isaacson, *Steve Jobs* (Simon & Schuster, 2011).

50 Stephen R. Covey, *The Speed of Trust* (Free Press, 2006).

51 Paul J. Zak, *Trust Factor: The Science of Creating High-Performance Companies* (AMACOM, 2017).

52 "Thomas A. Edison Papers," Rutgers–New Brunswick School of Arts and Sciences, edison.rutgers.edu, accessed January 19, 2026, https://edison.rutgers.edu.

53 Isaacson, *Steve Jobs.*

54 OpenAI, "GPT-4 Technical Report," cdn.openai.com, March 27, 2023, https://cdn.openai.com/papers/gpt-4.pdf.

55 Parrish, "#41 Tobi Lütke."

56 Eric Berger, "SpaceX pushing iterative design process, accepting failure to go fast," ARS Technica, February 21, 2020, https://arstechnica.com/science/2020/02/elon-musk-says-spacex-driving-toward-orbital-starship-flight-in-2020/.

57 McCraty, *Science of the Heart.*

58 Zak, *Trust Factor.*

59 Department of the Army, "ADP 6-0: Mission Command," May 2012, https://adamdrake.com/static/ADP-6-0-Mission-Command.pdf.

60   Gary Klein, "Performing a Project Premortem," Harvard Business Review, September 2007, https://hbr.org/2007/09/performing-a-project-premortem.

61   Zach Bush, "Remember Ourselves as a Murmuration," Awakin.org, accessed January 27, 2026, https://www.awakin.org/v2/read/view.php?tid=2751.

62   Porges, *The Polyvagal Theory*; Woo Woolley, et al. "Evidence for a Collective Intelligence Factor in the Performance of Human Groups."

63   McCraty, *Science of the Heart*.

64   Woolley, et al. "Evidence for a Collective Intelligence Factor in the Performance of Human Groups," 686–688.

65   Amy Edmondson, "Psychological Safety and Learning Behavior in Work Teams," *Administrative Science Quarterly* 44 (1999): 350–383.

66   Bo Cowgill, Justin Wolfers, and Eric Zitzewitz, "Using Prediction Markets to Track Information Flows: Evidence from Google," Dartmouth college, January 2008.

67   Michael Mankins and Mark Gottfredson, "Strategy-Making in Turbulent Times," Bain & Company, August 2022, https://www.bain.com/insights/strategy-making-in-turbulent-times-hbr/.

68   "Make faster, better decisions," McKinsey & Company, accessed January 27, 2026, https://www.mckinsey.com/capabilities/people-and-organizational-performance/our-insights/make-faster-better-decisions.

69   "Navigating the rising tide of uncertainty: PwC's 23rd Annual Global CEO Survey – Singapore Report," pwc.com, 2020, https://www.pwc.com/sg/en/publications/assets/sg-ceo-survey-2020.pdf.

70   Jeffrey P. Bezos, "To our shareholders" (2014 PDF), amazon.com, accessed January 13, 2026, https://s2.q4cdn.com/299287126/files/doc_financials/annual/2015-Letter-to-Shareholders.PDF.

71   Peter Senge, *The Fifth Discipline: The Art and Practice of the Learning Organization* (Doubleday, 1990).

72   David Pogue, "Netflix's Red Envelope Revolution," *New York Times*, March 15, 2007, https://www.nytimes.com/2007/03/15/technology/15pogue.html.

73 Aamy F. T. Arnsten, "Stress Signalling Pathways that Impair Prefrontal Cortex Structure and Function," *Nature Reviews Neuroscience* 10, no. 6 (2009): 410–422.

74 Grant S. Shields, Matthew A. Sazma, and Andrew P. Yonelinas, "The Effects of Acute Stress on Core Executive Functions," *Psychological Bulletin* 142, no. 6 (2016): 621–664.

75 Porges, *The Polyvagal Theory.*

76 Daniel J. Siegel, *Pocket Guide to Interpersonal Neurobiology: An Integrative Handbook of the Mind* (W. W. Norton & Company, 2012).

77 Max Bazerman, "The Power of Noticing: What the Best Leaders See," Harvard Business School, 2014, https://pmc.ncbi.nlm.nih.gov/articles/PMC5134841/.

78 Edward Tenner, "The Era of the Efficiency Trap," *Harvard Business Review 89,* no. 9 (September 2011): 32–33.

79 Bezos, "To our shareholders" (2014 PDF).

80 Geoffrey Garrett, "Distributed Decision-Making and Innovation Speed: Lessons from the Next-Normal," Wharton Global Initiatives/Knowledge at Wharton, 2020–2021, accessed January 29, 2026, https://nextforge.com/getting-to-your-next-normal/.

81 Mankins and Gottfredson, "Strategy-Making in Turbulent Times."

82 James Manyika, et al., "Jobs Lost, Jobs Gained: What the future of work will mean for jobs, skills, and wages," McKinsey & Company, November 28, 2017, https://www.mckinsey.com/featured-insights/future-of-work/jobs-lost-jobs-gained-what-the-future-of-work-will-mean-for-jobs-skills-and-wages.

83 "How Will AI Affect the Global Workforce?" Goldman Sachs, August 13, 2025, https://www.goldmansachs.com/insights/articles/how-will-ai-affect-the-global-workforce.

84 Julian F. Thayer, Fredrik Åhs, Mats Fredrikson, John J. Sollers III, and Tor D. Wager, "A meta-analysis of heart rate variability and neuroimaging studies," *Neuroscience & Biobehavioral Reviews* 26, no. 2 (2012): 747–756..

85 McCraty, *Science of the Heart.*

86 McCraty, *Science of the Heart.*

87   Jim Collins, *Good to Great* (Harper Business, 2001).

88   https://views4you.com/ai-tools-usage-statistics-report-2025

89   World Economic Forum, "Future of Jobs Report 2023," weforum.org, April 30, 2023, https://www.weforum.org/publications/the-future-of-jobs-report-2023/.

90   Geoff Woods, *The AI-Driven Leader: Becoming a Thought Partner with Intelligence* (AI Thought Leadership, 2024).

91   Woods, *The AI-Driven Leader.*

92   Woods, *The AI-Driven Leader.*

93   Stanley McChrystal, *Team of Teams: New Rules of Engagement for a Complex World* (Portfolio, 2014).

94   McChrystal, *Team of Teams.*

95   David Rock and Christine Cox, "SCARF in 2012: updating the social neuroscience of collaborating with others," *NeuroLeadership Journal* 4, https://clubrunner.blob.core.windows.net/00000003364/en-us/files/homepage/scarf-document/SCARF-in-2012.pdf; Al H. Ringleb, David Rock, and Chris Ancona, "NeuroLeadership in 2011 and 2012, *NeuroLeadership Journal* 4, https://www.researchgate.net/profile/Al-Ringleb-2/publication/263298268_NeuroLeadership_in_2011_and_2012/links/0f31753a8144a7b602000000/NeuroLeadership-in-2011-and-2012.pdf.

96   "Understand team effectiveness," Google Re:Work, accessed January 19, 2026, https://rework.withgoogle.com/intl/en/guides/understanding-team-effectiveness.

97   McChrystal, *Team of Teams.*

98   Woods, *The AI-Driven Leader.*

99   Gene Kim, Jez Humble, and Nicole Forsgren, *Accelerate: Building and Scaling High Performing Technology Organizations* (DORA Research, 2018).

100   John Doerr, *Measure What Matters* (Portfolio, 2018).

101   Michale c. Mankins and Eric Garton, *Time, Talent, Energy: Overcome Organizational Drag and Unleash Your Team's Productive Power* (Harvard Business Review Press, 2017).

102 Lao-tzu, *Tao-te Ching,* trans. James Legge, classics.mit.edu, https://classics.mit.edu/Lao/taote.html.

103 Christiaan Huygens, *Horologium Oscillatorium: The Sympathetic Motion of Pendulums* (Paris, 1673).

104 Itzhak Bentov, *Stalking the Wild Pendulum: On the Mechanics of Consciousness* (Dutton, 1977).

105 McCraty, *Science of the Heart.*

106 Porges, *The Polyvagal Theory.*

107 Csikszentmihalyi, M. (1990). *Flow: The Psychology of Optimal Experience.* Harper & Row.

108 Ruth Ann Atchley, David L. Strayer, Paul and Atchley, "Creativity in the Wild: Improving Creative Reasoning through Immersion in Natural Settings," *PloS One* 7, no. 12 (2012): e51474.

109 Bentov, *Stalking the Wild Pendulum*

110 McCraty, *Science of the Heart.*

111 Porges, *The Polyvagal Theory.*

112 Jeremy Utley and Perry Klebahn, *Ideaflow: The Only Business Metric That Matters* (Portfolio, 2022).

113 McKinsey & Company, "The State of Organizations 2023: Transforming Performance through People and Rhythm," mckinsey.com, accessed January 13, 2026, https://www.mckinsey.com/~/media/mckinsey/business%20functions/people%20and%20organizational%20performance/our%20insights/the%20state%20of%20organizations%202023/the-state-of-organizations-2023.pdf.

114 Ruth Feldman, "The Neurobiology of Human Attachments," *Trends in Cognitive Sciences* 21, no. 2 (2016): 80–99.

115 David R. Hawkins, *Power vs. Force: The Hidden Determinants of Human Behavior* (Hay House, 1995).

116 Hawkins, *Power vs. Force.*

117 McCraty, *Science of the Heart.*

118 Hawkins, *Power vs. Force.*

119 Joe Dispenza, *Becoming Supernatural: How Common People Are Doing the Uncommon* (Hay House, 2019).

120   Antonio Damasio, *Descartes' Error: Emotion, Reason, and the Human Brain* (Putnam, 1994).

121   Lisa Feldman Barrett, *How Emotions Are Made: The Secret Life of the Brain* (Houghton Mifflin Harcourt, 2017).

122   Howard Gardner, *Creating Minds: An Anatomy of Creativity* (Basic Books, 1999).

123   Porges, *The Polyvagal Theory*.

124   Utley and Klebahn, *Ideaflow*.

125   Mark Epstein, *Thoughts Without a Thinker: Psychotherapy from a Buddhist Perspective* (Basic Books, 1995).

126   Albert Einstein, "Letter to Lyn Osborn regarding unified field theory," Albert Einstein Papers, Princeton University Archives, 1944.

127   McCraty, *Science of the Heart*.

128   Issac Newton, *The Principia: Mathematical Principles of Natural Philosophy*, trans. I. Bernard Cohen and Anne Whitman (University of California Press, 1999).

129   M. Planck, "On the Law of Distribution of Energy in the Normal Spectrum," *Annalen der Physik*, no. 4 (1901): 553–562.

130   Albert Einstein, "On a Heuristic Point of View Concerning the Production and Transformation of Light," *Annalen der Physik*, no. 17 (1905): 132–148.

131   Thomas Young, "On the Nature of Light and Colours," *Philosophical Transactions of the Royal Society of London*, no. 92 (1802): 12–48.

132   Richard Feynman, *The Feynman Lectures on Physics*, vol. 3 (Addison Wesley, 1971).

133   Albert Einstein, Boris Podolsky, and Nathan Rosen, "Can Quantum-Mechanical Description of Physical Reality Be Considered Complete?" *Physical Review* 47, no. 10 (1935): 777–780.

134   J. S. Bell, "On the Einstein Podolsky Rosen Parado," *Physics Physique Fizika* 1, no. 3 (1964): 195–200.

135   "Alain Aspect: Banquet speech," The Nobel Prize, nobelprize.org, December 10, 2022, https://www.nobelprize.org/prizes/physics/2022/aspect/speech/.

136 Ludwig von Bertalanffy, *General System Theory: Foundations, Development, Applications* (George Braziller, 1968).

137 Norbert Wiener, *Cybernetics: Or Control and Communication in the Animal and the Machine* (MIT Press, 1948).

138 Edward N. Lorenz, E "Deterministic Nonperiodic Flow," *Journal of the Atmospheric Sciences* 20, no. 2 (1963): 130–141.

139 Tara Swart, *The Source: The Secrets of the Universe, the Science of the Brain* (HarperCollins, 2019).

www.ingramcontent.com/pod-product-compliance
Lightning Source LLC
Chambersburg PA
CBHW030514210326
41597CB00013B/907